WOODLAND BIRDS

of North America

WOODLAND BIRDS

of North America

A Guide to Observation, Understanding and Conservation

Scott Leslie

KEY PORTER BOOKS

Library and Archives Canada Cataloguing in Publication

Leslie, Scott, 1963–
    Woodland birds of North America : a guide to observing, understanding and conservation /
Scott Leslie.

ISBN 978-1-55263-922-1

    1. Forest birds—North America—Identification.   2. Bird watching—North America—
Guidebooks. I. Title.

QL677.79.F67L47 2008   598.097   C2007-901957-9

ONTARIO ARTS COUNCIL
CONSEIL DES ARTS DE L'ONTARIO

The publisher gratefully acknowledges the support of the Canada Council for the Arts and the
Ontario Arts Council for its publishing program. We acknowledge the support of the
Government of Ontario through the Ontario Media Development Corporation's Ontario Book
Initiative.

We acknowledge the financial support of the Government of Canada through the Book
Publishing Industry Development Program (BPIDP) for our publishing activities.

Conservation status maps courtesy of NatureServe. 2006. NatureServe Explorer: An online
encyclopedia of life [web application]. Version 6.1. NatureServe, Arlington, Virginia. Available
at www.natureserve.org/explorer.

Range maps courtesy of Ridgely, R.S., T.F. Allnutt, T. Brooks, D.K. McNicol, D.W. Mehlman,
B.E. Young, and J.R. Zook. 2005. Digital Distribution Maps of the Birds of the Western
Hemisphere, version 2.1. NatureServe, Arlington, Virginia, USA.

Key Porter Books Limited
Six Adelaide Street East, Tenth Floor
Toronto, Ontario
Canada M5C 1H6

NatureServe

www.keyporter.com

Text Design: Marijke Friesen
Formatting: Jean Lightfoot Peters
Photograph of Northern Goshawk on page 33 provided by Douglas Herr
Printed and bound in China

08 09 10 11 12 6 5 4 3 2 1

In memory of my mother
Lona B. Leslie

TABLE OF

CONTENTS

PREFACE

The sounds and sights of nature are becoming more difficult to experience as cities become larger and louder, our lives grow busier, we spend ever more hours in automobiles and our fascination with cell phones and other electronic gadgets grows. Chance moments of quiet observation in the natural environment have been all but removed from our day-to-day experience. They are still there to be enjoyed, however. You just have to work a little harder for them. By taking a short trip to the nearest brushy lot, wooded park or wild ravine you should discover a variety of woodland birds. One doesn't have to travel to a large wilderness area to get acquainted with wild nature. In wooded habitats across North America, from great forests to inauspicious thickets, untold billions of these generally small feathered friends tirelessly *warble, whistle, cheep* and *chirp* their way through the spring and summer seasons. As if their melodious songs weren't enough, their plumage and ceaseless activity creates a *visual* music. A veritable rainbow of colors—red, green, blue, yellow, orange, black, white and practically every combination thereof—is offered up for those willing to look for it, for these sights and sounds fill the hundreds of millions of acres of forests and other treed, bushy and shrubby habitats on the continent. Woodland birds are never that far away, as long as one is willing to look and listen for them.

I hope this book succeeds as an effective guide to the life histories of many of our woodland bird species, and that it will inspire you to go out and experience the precious diversity of life in the larger world of nature that still survives outside of our own.

THE WOODS ARE FULL OF BIRDS

Did you ever chance to hear the midnight flight of birds passing through the air and darkness overhead, in countless armies, changing their early or late summer habitat? It is something not to be forgotten.

WALT WHITMAN

Quork, quork, quork. The call of ravens draws my gaze upward into the canopy of 150-year-old sugar maples and yellow birch. Through a hole in the roof of the forest where a large tree once stood, I watch the shiny black birds mirthfully tumble and roll across the sky in a renewal of their lifelong pair bond. Invisible in its cryptic plumage among the saplings and newly emerging woodland plants, a nearby ovenbird belts out *tee-cher, tee-cher, tee-cher* in a crescendo that becomes so loud I wonder how such a big sound can come out of so small a thing. A chorus of warblers, thrushes and vireos, each singing its own unique and timeless song, forms the musical background that is the hallmark of this and other North American woodlands coming to life in the spring.

The black-and-white warbler is one of scores of species lending its beauty to North America's woodlands

Woodland birds are often more difficult to observe than birds that live in open habitats such as wetlands and grasslands. Ecological niches for forest birds are located in 3 dimensions, from on the ground to perhaps 100 feet or more up among the leaves and twigs of large trees, as well as everywhere in between. That's a lot of hiding places. It isn't always easy to appreciate how pervasive bird life is in most woodlands, but if one pays close attention, watching and listening carefully, it will soon become apparent.

Each spring we are eager to welcome home literally billions of birds to our forests to join those stalwart resident species that stay on year-round and do not migrate. Birds of every shape, size and color appear at this time of year as though conjured out of the ether by the lengthening daylight. They herald the rebirth of life in a winter-weary land as they fill the hundreds of millions of acres of forests and woodlands with color and song. All manner of birds, from the tiny ruby-throated hummingbird to the magnificent red-tailed hawk, return from distant points in the hemisphere to find, with unerring accuracy, a breeding territory that for some species may be smaller than an acre. After a perilous journey of thousands of miles through storms, cold weather and the threat of predators, migrant woodland birds are emaciated, spent and hungry, having burned all their available fat. Their arrival coincides with the hatching of insects, the appearance of buds and blossoms and the emergence of rodents from their winter slumber: the smorgasbord of nutriment is set for another breeding season. Is it any wonder that migrant songbirds bubble with the melodies of springtime? They are happy just to have a meal and put on a little weight!

A male ruby-throated hummingbird shows off the feature for which it is named

In marked contrast to the survival strategy of migrants are the year-round residents—the chickadees, nuthatches, kinglets, ravens, owls and others—that endure winter's cold and relative lack of food. This strategy may at first appear the more difficult of the two, and maybe it is, but unlike migratory species, year-round residents avoid two gruelling journeys every year that are fraught with pitfalls, as well as the ever-present threat that their tropical wintering habitat will be destroyed. In the spring, these year-round birds are no less charged than the migrants are with a new vitality as they prepare to breed.

About 40 percent, or approximately 1.5 *billion* acres, of North America is covered by forests and woodlands of some kind. They are the dominant habitats in areas where average summer temperatures are at least 50°F. This includes the enormous swath of boreal forest in the North, the great deciduous woodlands of the eastern temperate zone, eastern coastal plain forests, the northern hardwood forests of the mid-latitude Northeast, the cordilleran forests of the western mountains and the great northwestern coastal forests, among others. And many wooded areas, especially those that are located in human-altered or heavily populated landscapes, defy being pigeonholed into a neat category.

Virtually every one of those billion-plus acres that make up the vast tapestry of North American forests is at some time during the year home to hundreds of individual birds. The continent's bird population is staggering in the tens of billions, and its ecosystems are diverse. Except for the enormous boreal forest, which is quite ecologically homogeneous, there is a great

A black-capped Chickadee in flight

variety of forest types from east to west, each with its own distinctive avian community.

Hundreds of species of birds depend on these myriad woodlands for their survival. Generalist species such as the common raven, the robin, the black-capped chickadee and the dark-eyed junco, to name just a few, can survive in a broad array of forest types comprising hundreds of millions of acres throughout the continent. On the other hand, many species have relatively narrow habitat requirements. For example, the blackpoll warbler needs

The Florida scrub-jay is one of the most endangered birds in North America

dense spruce and fir forest and the ovenbird is mostly limited to mature hardwoods. Despite having fairly specific habitat requirements, the places that many such species depend on are still fairly widespread and accordingly most of their populations appear secure. Unfortunately, birds with *highly* specialized habitat requirements are often vulnerable to serious population declines and possible extinctions. They are very sensitive to habitat loss and account for a large percentage of the species that appear on endangered lists. These birds simply had less suitable habitat to begin with and the continuing destruction of what little remains has pushed some of them into an ecological corner. Examples are the

Florida scrub-jay, the southwestern *extimus* subspecies of willow flycatcher and the verdin, each of which can survive only in a very specific habitat type. This has resulted in a very restricted range for the first 2 species. Both are threatened with extinction. The verdin, though wider ranging and still common, has nevertheless has had an 85 percent decline in its population in recent decades.

Perched low in dense woods, this red-shouldered hawk is on the lookout for prey on the ground below

Periods of decline are nothing new for birds. At several times in the past large numbers of them became extinct for various reasons. Three million years ago 25 percent of all bird species were wiped out because of climate change. But the difference now is that the agent of change, *Homo sapiens*, is not a random geological or climatic event, but a thinking being that has the intelligence and a (hopefully) strong enough self-preservation instinct not to destroy the natural world. Of the 650 or so bird species that breed in North America today, almost one-third are declining, many of them dependent on woodlands. There are many reasons for the declines: outright habitat loss and forest fragmentation both here and on neotropical wintering grounds; hunting by domestic cats (killing a staggering 1 *billion* songbirds per year or 3 *million per day* in North America—this is second only to habitat loss); hunting by humans; pest control; pollution; collisions with automobiles and buildings; and global warming.

If you listen carefully, you'll notice that lately our woodlands are a little quieter, a little less "birdy." Nowadays, birdsong doesn't always fill the woods. It's there, but it's diminished. Though the year round resident species are holding their own quite well, migratory birds are dwindling. Saving migrant songbirds may be one of the most difficult tasks facing North American conservationists and bird lovers. Allowing a further decline will not only diminish the exuberance of bird life, it will impoverish entire forest ecosystems that depend on birds.

The species accounts and photographs that follow are meant to inform and delight. I also hope that they will inspire the reader to take an interest in the welfare of North America's woodland birds.

A note about the birds included in this book: With literally hundreds of species dependent on North America's woodlands, it is impractical to include them all in a book of this type. The species presented here are a cross section of birds found in the continent's woodlands.

WOODLAND HABITATS: A VARIETY OF HOMES FOR BILLIONS OF BIRDS

The thick spruce forest was a welcome respite from the hot sun that was beating down on the highway where we parked the car. The densely needled foliage created cool shade, reducing the light reaching the forest floor to a dull green luminance just strong enough to support the most shade-resistant plants. This resulted in an understory that was relatively open and easy to traverse. We were penetrating deep into the woods to observe a creature that had reached an almost mythical status in my mind: the northern goshawk.

The reputation of this powerful raptor, a favorite of falconers throughout the centuries for its fearlessness and speed in the hunt, had drawn me here. I had never before seen one, so a devoted naturalist was taking me to see its nest. There was complete silence as we walked on the soft mossy ground, while slowly negotiating between the trunks of fir and spruce. My anticipation grew as we drew closer. "We're almost there, she'll see us soon, so get ready to defend yourself," he whispered. Ahead, a large spruce stood beside a small open patch in the woods. The nest sat on a high branch near the trunk. There was no hawk to be seen. Tapping me on the shoulder, my companion put his finger to his lips to signal me not to speak, then pointed to the bird resting on a heavy limb about 20 feet below the nest. Before I was able to focus my eyes, the goshawk left the branch and swept down toward us in a blur, hitting me square on the top of my flinching head with her sharp talons and knocking my hat off. Her ferocity in protecting the eggs was impressive. In a display of superb adaptation to her habitat, the goshawk twisted and turned as she slalomed and squeezed a nearly 4-foot wingspan between trees that were only a few feet apart. She was the apex predator in this dim world of conifers, and her species reigned as such across much of the northern half of North America's forest. We had disturbed her enough, so we made a hasty retreat and left her to her kingdom.

The northern goshawk resides in perhaps what many North Americans think of as the archetypal forest: the vast coniferous and mixed woodlands that stretch across the northern United States and much of Canada. But this habitat, wide ranging as it is, is at one end of a broad spectrum of woodland habitats used by birds throughout North America.

As mobile as they are, birds are able to live in virtually every available wooded ecosystem in North America: from a goshawk hunting the northern boreal forest to green jays foraging the dry scrub woods of southern Texas to the fox sparrow singing its heart out on a Douglas fir sapling in the Rockies. Spread far and wide across the continent, woodland birds occupy every conceivable forest niche.

Depending on the scale used and how narrowly we define them, there are over 100 kinds of woodland ecosystems in North America. However, it's generally more practical to break habitats into more broadly defined types. There are nearly 700 species of trees in Canada and the United States (coincidentally, about the same number of bird species also inhabit the continent) from small shrubs to the giant sequoia. The forests of no 2 regions are identical and except where geographical barriers such as mountain ranges, prairies and deserts exist, there is a continuous morphing of one forest type into another as one travels through them. The diversity of species generally decreases from south to north and from sea level to high altitudes as temperatures influence the amount of food that is available to support the biological community.

BOREAL FOREST OR TAIGA

Also called the northern coniferous forest, the boreal is the largest continuous forest in North America. It stretches in a giant swath across most of Canada and into Alaska. To its north extend the vast expanses of Arctic tundra. Made up almost entirely of softwoods such as spruce, fir, pine and larch, with a few cold-tolerant hardwoods thrown in for good measure, it is still largely untouched and inaccessible. Studies suggest that the boreal forest may support up to 60 percent (in absolute numbers, not diversity)

Part of the great boreal forest that stretches across North America

of nesting birds in Canada and 30 percent of the total population on the continent. The vast majority of birds that breed here are migratory. Warblers, vireos, finches and the like depend on abundant insect life and long northern summer days to raise their broods before fleeing as the late-summer days grow shorter at the approach of a chill autumn and brutal winter. Only a relatively few species are year-round residents, including the common raven, the gray jay, boreal chickadee and the northern hawk owl, among others.

PACIFIC COAST FOREST

Running in a narrow ribbon along the northwestern North American coast from southern Alaska and northern British Columbia to northern California, the Pacific Coast forest is made up of some of the most magnificent stands of trees on Earth. Enormous Douglas fir, redwood, western hemlock, sitka spruce and western red cedar dominate an ecosystem that remained largely unscathed during the last ice age. Known as a temperate rain forest, it is characterized by very high rainfall and mild winters. It is predominantly coniferous, with some notable deciduous trees such as big-leaf maple, red alder and vine maple. Breeding birds include the purple finch, dark-eyed junco, barred owl and the red-breasted nuthatch.

CORDILLERAN FOREST

The predominant forest habitat of the mountains of western North America, the cordilleran covers the Rockies, the Sierras and the Cascades, as well as smaller mountain ranges. Summers are warm and dry and winters cold and wet with considerable snowfall in the more northerly sections as well as in higher elevations in the south. It contains the most diverse assemblage of coniferous trees on the

Cordilleran forest and pinyon-juniper woodlands

continent, with lodgepole and ponderosa pine, white fir and California red fir and giant sequoia, as well as many others. Deciduous trees are also quite diverse and species such as oak produce many seeds that are an important source of food for the diverse bird life. Typical breeding residents are evening grosbeaks, yellow-rumped warblers and brown creepers, among others. With an abundance of seeds, acorns and nuts, the cordilleran is also important to scores of migrating species.

PINYON-JUNIPER WOODLANDS
Growing where there is little water, the pinyon-juniper woodland is found throughout the Great Basin area of the southwestern United States. Most trees are small, cone-bearing species that are usually scattered in clumps and are adapted to the dry conditions that prevail here. Bird diversity is quite low and includes breeders such as the western scrub jay, the red-tailed hawk and the canyon wren. The abundant juniper berries attract berry-eating migrants in winter, such as American robins.

OPEN OAK WOODLAND
California's dry foothill country (and also to a limited extent in parts of Arizona, New Mexico and Colorado) is dominated by open woodlands of several species of evergreen live oaks, laurels and tan oak. These park-like woodlands are a combination of patchily distributed trees interspersed by rolling grasslands. Acorn-loving birds such as acorn woodpeckers and western scrub-jays are relatively common. A similar oak-pine habitat in southeast Arizona and southwest New Mexico supports southwestern specialty species such as the yellow-eyed junco and the Mexican jay. This area is also the center of hummingbird diversity in North America.

EASTERN MIXED FOREST
Stretching from the eastern edge of the midwest Prairies to Nova Scotia and south into northern Pennsylvania, the eastern mixed forest is a large transition zone between the coniferous boreal forest to the north and the deciduous forests to the south. In fall, multicolored hardwoods and dark green conifers create a rich natural

Eastern mixed forest with a variety of deciduous and coniferous trees

tapestry on the rolling landscape. Dominant tree species include sugar maple, American beech, yellow birch, American basswood, red oak, white pine, eastern hemlock and others. This great variety of relatively tall trees, both coniferous and deciduous, towering over an understory that is richly layered with shrubs and other vegetation, provides a large variety of avian habitats. Both migrant and breeding bird life is particularly diverse here and includes wood warblers such as the black-throated green warbler, the black-and-white warbler and the American redstart. Various species of thrushes, vireos, owls, hawks and flycatchers, among others, also make the eastern mixed forest home.

OAK-HICKORY FOREST

Formerly the domain of the mighty American chestnut, this region is now dominated by various deciduous species, especially red, bur and white oak, and shagbark and mocker-nut hickory. Generally dry with widely spaced large trees and a low undergrowth of shrubs, these forests thrive where the 4 seasons are near equal in length and moderate to high precipitation is evenly distributed throughout the year. They are important to a large array of breeding species such as ruffed grouse, northern flicker, blue jay, red-shouldered hawk and many woodland songbirds. The abundant acorns and seed crops attract many migrant species in both spring and fall.

SOUTHERN APPALACHIAN FOREST

Covering the ancient Appalachians and surrounding lands from southern Pennsylvania to Georgia is the southern Appalachian forest. One of the most diverse plant communities on the continent, some 1,600 species of wildflowers and 130 species of trees grow here in rich soils. More virgin forest exists here (in places like the Great Smoky Mountains) than anywhere else in eastern North America. The great elevation change, from deep river valleys to the bald mountaintops, has allowed a range of plants from tropical to Arctic species to thrive. As is the case with oak-hickory forests, the 4 seasons are nearly equal in length and precipitation falls evenly throughout the year. Because of an abundance of insects, acorns and seeds, both migrant and breeding bird species are diverse. Numbered among them are the pileated woodpecker, northern cardinal, brown thrasher and ovenbird.

Eastern oak-hickory forest

SOUTHERN PINE-OAK FOREST

This open forest of pines runs from eastern Texas across the top of the Gulf of Mexico to Florida and north to Virginia. Shortleaf, longleaf, loblolly and slash pine are the predominant species, along with hawthorns, saw palmetto and several oak species. Grasses rather than shrubs are the dominant ground species. Frequent fires maintain the composition of the forest. The soil tends to be dry and poorly drained, which results in the creation of swamp forests of cypress and tupelo, and boggy areas known as pocasins. Bird life of the southern pine-oak forest is distinctive and varied with such breeders as the great-crested flycatcher and tufted titmouse, and in the swamps, the northern parula. A southern extension of this forest is the remnant oak scrub of the Florida peninsula where the imperiled Florida scrub-jay is fighting for survival.

*Southern
bottomland
forest*

FLORIDA HAMMOCKS

The woodlands of southernmost Florida, including those in the Everglades, grow on elevated "islands" of drier ground surrounded by marshes, wet prairies, mangroves and cypress swamps. These hammocks, as they are known, support some subtropical breeding bird species at the northern limit of their ranges. They are also the only wintering grounds in North America for several species of northern breeding warblers, including the Cape May warbler, the black-throated green warbler and the black-throated blue warbler.

RIPARIAN WOODLANDS

Although not specific to any one region, riparian woodlands are key environments for birds throughout the continent because their proximity to water allows a richness of plant life often not found in adjacent areas. Especially vital in grasslands and the arid southwest, where they are often the only treed environments where both water and shade are available, riparian zones support an abundance and diversity of bird life that is far out of proportion to their actual physical extent. The "green corridors" of the American desert are crucial migratory stopovers for millions of birds as they make their way north for the breeding season and back again in the fall. As these cottonwood, willow and other linear forests disappear, it becomes more difficult for migrants to complete their journeys. Unfortunately, the riparian habitat is often under great development pressure, especially in the southwestern United States, where water is in perennial short supply. Year-round residents that are imperiled include a subspecies of the willow flycatcher and the Bell's vireo of California.

A "sky island" open oak mountain forest in southeastern Arizona, the center of hummingbird diversity in North America

INTRODUCTION TO THE SPECIES ACCOUNTS

It is not enough to know how to simply identify a bird. Just as important, and perhaps even more so, is an understanding of the *way* it lives. What habitats does it prefer? How does it feed and get around? What does it sound like? What does it eat? How does it nest and rear its young? Does it migrate and, if so, when? Who are its closest relatives? And perhaps, the most important question of all in light of the increasing pressure being put on the Earth's ecosystems by humans: How healthy is its population?

There are 92 species in this book, a representative selection of the diversity of woodland birds. The species accounts are divided into 17 main groupings, each one a chapter. Each account features photographs of and range maps for each bird as well as a natural history that is divided into 9 sections. For the most part, the 9 sections relate to birds during the breeding season. For example, under "Appearance" I describe breeding plumage, and in the habitat section, I describe the environment where the bird breeds and not where it winters. For some of the more threatened species a conservation status map is also included. The "Species Status Overall for North America" under the "Conservation Concerns" section for each species, as well as the range maps and conservation maps, are derived from NatureServe.org. This nonprofit collaboration of Canadian, U.S., Latin American and Caribbean conservation groups and agencies provides some of the most current and accurate data available to those working in the field of conservation biology.

A note about some terminology in the species accounts:

- *Altricial* young are born helpless, without feathers or down, often with eyes closed and are totally dependent on their parents.
- *Semi-altricial* young are born with eyes either open or closed and are down covered but unable to leave the nest. They are completely dependent on parents.
- *Precocial* young are born with eyes open, covered in down and are able to leave the nest within 2 days. They may be partially dependent or not dependent on parents to survive.
- *Hawking* is a hunting method where the bird flies out from a perch to capture flying insects.
- *Polygamous* mating occurs when both males and females may have two or more mates.
- *Polygynous* mating occurs when a male breeds with 2 or more mates.

RANGE MAP LEGEND

Permanent Resident

Breeding Resident

Nonbreeding Resident

Passage Migrant

Uncertain Status

Introduced

Vagrant

CONSERVATION MAP LEGEND

Presumed Extirpated

Possibly Extirpated

Critically Imperiled

Imperiled

Vulnerable

Apparently Secure

Secure

Not Ranked/
Under Review

DEFINITIONS OF CONSERVATION
MAP LEGEND TERMS

Presumed Extirpated: Species is believed to be extirpated from the nation or state/province. Not located despite intensive searches of historical sites and other appropriate habitat, and virtually no likelihood that it will be rediscovered.

Possibly Extirpated (Historical): Species occurred historically in the nation or state/province, and there is some possibility that it may be rediscovered.

Critically Imperiled: Critically imperiled in the nation or state/province because of extreme rarity (often 5 or fewer occurrences) or because of some factor(s) such as very steep declines making it especially vulnerable to extirpation from the state/province.

Imperiled: Imperiled in the nation or state/province because of rarity due to a very restricted range, very few populations (often 20 or fewer), steep declines or other factors making it very vulnerable to extirpation from the nation or state/province.

Vulnerable: Vulnerable in the nation or state/province due to a restricted range, relatively few populations (often 80 or fewer), recent and widespread declines or other factors making it vulnerable to extirpation.

Apparently Secure: Uncommon but not rare; some cause for long-term concern due to declines or other factors.

Secure: Common, widespread and abundant in the nation or state/province.

Not Yet Ranked: Nation or state/province conservation status not yet assessed.

NORTHERN GOSHAWK

(Accipiter gentilis)

A northern goshawk waits patiently deep within the forest for prey to happen by

The largest hawk of the deep woods is an efficient, powerful predator and a fierce protector of its nest, often striking painfully at intruding humans with its sharp talons.

APPEARANCE

Length: 21 inches. *Wingspan:* 41 inches. Relatively heavy-bodied; back and wings are uniformly gray; long, rounded wings and tail; black crown and patches behind eyes; heavy white "eyebrow" and orange-red eye; white underparts with gray mottling. The female is considerably larger than the male.

HABITAT

Inhabits boreal and temperate coniferous and mixed coniferous-deciduous forests, open woodlands, northern riparian woods. Prefers habitat with large, mature trees.

BEHAVIOR

Hunts by taking short search flights through the forest, making frequent stops to perch and scan for prey. Most prey live on or near

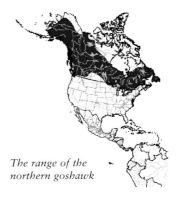

The range of the northern goshawk

the ground. After a silent, accelerating approach glide (doesn't beat wings during final swoop), it captures prey by striking with power-ful talons. Hunts and captures birds in midair. Often crashes through branches and bushes during pursuit and will sometimes enter the water to capture animals. Is efficient at walking and run-ning on the ground. Flight is very rapid, with great maneuverability on strong, quickly beating wings alternating with glides. Occasionally soars on thermals in the manner of a red-tailed hawk.

CALLS

Commonly heard alarm call is a harsh *kee-kee-kee*. Female gives a high, mournful *kee-yah*.

FOOD

Eats a wide variety of prey. Diet includes squirrels, rabbits and hares, other rodents, birds such as crows, ducks, grouse, flickers, among others, and occasionally insects and reptiles.

FAMILY LIFE

Monogamous pair; both sexes participate (more work done by the male) in building a platform nest of sticks and twigs and lining it with evergreen sprigs, grass, feathers, shreds of bark, then placing it in the crotch of a tree well off the ground. Nest is often located in the largest tree in an area. The typical clutch of 3 or 4 eggs is incubated by both sexes (female does more) for 36 to 42 days.

Semialtricial young remain in the nest for 41 to 43 days and are fed by both parents. One brood per year.

MIGRATION
Migratory biology is poorly known for this species. It appears that some populations are migratory. Most are year-round residents. Those that do migrate may be driven to wander by a lack of food. Spring migrants appear to arrive on breeding grounds from February to early May. Fall migration appears to occur from late August to early December.

CONSERVATION
CONCERNS
Species status overall in North America is only *apparently secure* in the United States and *secure* in Canada. No evidence of a decline, but may be declining in some areas due to logging operations. Listed as a "forest-sensitive species" by the United States Forest Service.

A conservation status map of the northern goshawk

RELATED SPECIES
Is 1 of 24 species of hawks belonging to the family *Accipitridae* in North America. The much smaller sharp-shinned hawk and the smaller Cooper's hawk belong to the same genus *Accipiter*.

RED-SHOULDERED HAWK

(Buteo lineatus)

*The rufous shoulder patches are
apparent on this red-shouldered hawk*

The red-shouldered hawk is often the most common hawk in its habitat. Here it will be found haunting its favorite swamps and woodlands while it waits to swoop on unsuspecting prey.

APPEARANCE

Length: 17 inches. *Wingspan:* 40 inches. A medium-sized hawk somewhat smaller and less robust than a red-tailed hawk; reddish shoulders; breast heavily barred in rusty red; yellow legs and feet; black-and-white checkered flight feathers. The cere (the area around the nostrils at the base of the bill) is a bright yellow. In flight look for the narrow white banding on the long tail as well as short, abrupt wing beats. From below, a translucent, finely barred crescent just before the wing's primary feathers is diagnostic.

HABITAT

Favored habitats include wet forests, riparian woodlands, wooded swamps, woodlots and agricultural areas with plenty of trees.

BEHAVIOR

Quite sedentary; unlike many of the other *Buteo* species, which tend to soar while hunting, the red-shouldered hawk usually hunts from a low perch, where it waits patiently for some unsuspecting prey to come by, then drops down to capture it. Also occasionally hunts by soaring and dropping on prey. Often hunts a forest edge along swamps, streams and other wet areas. Flight is rapid with stiff, beating wings alternating with gliding.

The range of the red-shouldered hawk

CALLS

A clearly uttered, powerful drawn-out *kee-yah, kee-yah,* repeated.

FOOD

Eats a very broad diet including small mammals, snakes, reptiles, frogs, snails, spiders, earthworms, crayfish, caterpillars and occasionally birds.

FAMILY LIFE

Monogamous pair; both the male and female participate in building a nest of sticks, twigs, strips of bark, leaves or moss and lining it with green leaves and other plant matter. The

An immature red-shouldered hawk

Red-shouldered hawks spend much of their time perched low in trees as they watch for prey

nest is placed in a tree, usually on a large branch close to the trunk at a height of 20–60 feet. The typical clutch of 3 eggs is incubated by both adults for 28 days. Semialtricial young remain in the nest for 35 to 40 days and are fed by both parents. Red-shouldered hawk pairs or their offspring may use the same nesting territory for decades. One brood per year.

MIGRATION

Migratory only in the northern portion of its breeding range. Spring birds generally arrive very early on the breeding grounds, usually in late February and March, and will leave on southward migration in October or November.

CONSERVATION CONCERNS

Species status overall in North America is *secure* in the United States and only *apparently secure* in Canada where it is a species of special concern due to its limited range. Like all species of hawks, the red-shouldered hawk was persecuted well into the twentieth century. Formerly known as the "hen hawk," it was wrongly thought to prey heavily on chickens and so was heavily hunted. Habitat loss also caused a decline in its numbers. The population appears stable, but ongoing destruction of its habitat and pollution pose a continued threat.

RELATED SPECIES

The red-shouldered hawk belongs to the genus *Buteo*, of which there are 8 other regularly occurring species in North America.

RED-TAILED HAWK

(Buteo jamaicensis)

A red-tailed hawk

When most people think of a hawk, they think of a red-tailed hawk. This beautiful, regal raptor is widely distributed throughout the continent and is commonly seen soaring high in the sky or perched on roadside trees.

APPEARANCE

Length: 19 inches. *Wingspan:* 49 inches. Is a large, heavy-bodied, overall brown to reddish-brown hawk. The tail's normally deep reddish brown is very apparent in flight; upperparts are generally dark with pale mottling; heavy hooked bill with yellow base and dark tip; underparts are lighter with dark streaking in a band across the belly. There is much individual variation within populations and between populations across its range.

HABITAT

Inhabits coniferous forests, deciduous forests, and mixed forests often with mature trees and adjacent open areas. Also lives in desert scrub, subarctic taiga, open woodlands, and agricultural areas with scattered trees.

The range of the red-tailed hawk

BEHAVIOR

Hunts primarily by visually scanning adjacent open country from an elevated perch. When prey is detected, the hawk alternately flaps and glides downward toward its target, thrusting its powerful talons out to grab the animal. Occasionally hunts by flying across open ground to scan for prey, and then attacking in the same manner as when it hunts from a perch. Hunts insects on the ground on foot. Takes smaller prey to a perch to be eaten; consumes larger prey at the site of the kill. Hops energetically across the ground when pursuing insect prey. Flight is strong with several powerful wing beats followed by gliding. Soars superbly on thermals with steady wings and a fanned tail.

CALLS

Most commonly heard call is a harsh, drawn out, descending *tcheeerrr*.

The red tail is apparent on this red-tailed hawk in flight

FOOD
Diet is primarily rodents, including voles, mice, rats, squirrels, chipmunks, rabbits and hares. Also takes birds such as pheasants, bobwhites, waterfowl and smaller passerines. Reptiles, amphibians, insects and fish are also eaten. Occasionally consumes carrion.

FAMILY LIFE
Monogamous pair; both sexes participate in building a large platform nest of sticks and twigs lined by strips of bark, grass, bits of evergreen and green leaves that is placed in the crotch of a large tree or on a ledge with a good view of the surrounding area. Occasionally uses an unused raptor's nest as a foundation upon which to build a new nest. The typical clutch of 2 or 3 eggs is incubated by both sexes (mostly the female) for 28 to 35 days. Semialtricial young remain in the nest for 42 to 46 days and are fed by both parents. One brood per year.

MIGRATION
Because of the broad distribution of the species, migration times vary widely. Birds arrive on spring breeding grounds as early as February and as late as June. Fall migration occurs between late August and early December.

CONSERVATION CONCERNS
Species status overall in North America is *secure* in the United States and Canada. Populations are stable or increasing throughout the continent.

RELATED SPECIES
One of 24 species of hawks belonging to the family *Accipitridae* in North America and 1 of 9 species belonging to the genus *Buteo*.

EASTERN SCREECH OWL

(Megascops asio)

An eastern screech-owl alert for prey at night

This little owl is often the most common bird of prey in our parks, gardens and residential areas.

APPEARANCE

Length: 8.5 inches. *Wingspan:* 20 inches. Overall color varies from gray to rufous red with finely patterned streaking and barring; large yellow eyes; ear tufts are sometimes not visible; dark "crescents" edge the sides of the face; short tail; pale bill helps differentiate this species from the nearly identical western screech-owl.

HABITAT
Lives in a broad variety of habitats, including deciduous, coniferous and mixed forests, parks, treed urban and residential areas, gardens, scrub, open woodlands and riparian habitats.

BEHAVIOR
Hunts by perching in a tree below the canopy of the forest, waiting for prey to come by (whether on the ground or in the air), and plummeting through the air to capture it in its talons. Usually

The range of the eastern screech owl

captures prey directly, but occasionally will hover near the ground to locate unseen prey. Also captures fish and tadpoles in shallow water in the same manner or by hopping out from the shore. Will walk on the ground under dense brush to roost. Vision is thought to be extremely acute. Flight is silent and buoyant on rapidly beating wings. Usually does not fly very far.

CALLS
Song, which has a tremulous, whinnying quality, is a series of descending whistles. Also performs a plaintive, quavering single-note call.

FOOD
Varies widely depending on location. Diet includes invertebrates such as insects, earthworms and crayfish. All types of vertebrates are taken, including small mammals, birds, amphibians and reptiles.

*An eastern
screech-owl
perched low on
a rock on the
forest floor*

FAMILY LIFE
Monogamous pair; the nest, located well off the ground, in a tree cavity, abandoned woodpecker hole or hollow stump lined with feathers, hair and debris from food; artificial nesting boxes are also used. The typical clutch of 4 or 5 eggs is incubated mostly by the female for 26 days. Semialtricial young remain in the nest for 28 days and are fed by both parents. One brood per year.

MIGRATION
Year-round resident.

CONSERVATION CONCERNS
Species status overall in North America is *secure* in the United States and Canada.

RELATED SPECIES
Is 1 of 18 species of owls belonging to the family *Strigidae* in North America. Closest relative is the western screech owl, which used to be considered the same species.

GREAT HORNED OWL
(*Bubo virginianus*)

A great horned owl

One of the most powerful birds of prey, this large, husky owl has one of the widest ranges of any bird in the western hemisphere and is found throughout most of North America, as well as large parts of Central and South America.

APPEARANCE
Length: 22 inches. *Wingspan:* 44 inches. A very large, heavyset bird; prominent ear tufts or "horns"; large yellow eyes surrounded by reddish facial disks; white chin and throat; upperparts are grayish overall with brown mottling; underparts are brownish with fine horizontal barring. Birds in the far northwest and southwest tend to be more grayish overall.

HABITAT

Inhabits coniferous forest, deciduous forest, mixed woodlands, grasslands, desert, swamps, suburban parkland and riparian woods. Is found in practically any reasonably natural habitat in North America except Arctic-alpine regions.

The range of the great horned owl

BEHAVIOR

Hunts primarily at night (but occasionally in the day) by perching adjacent to an open area and swooping on prey. Daytime ecological counterpart is the red-tailed hawk, which generally hunts the same species in the same habitats. Occasionally hunts in the manner of a short-eared owl or harrier by flying back and forth (known as quartering) over open areas such grasslands or sagebrush. Also known to walk along the ground stalking prey hidden in vegetation. Captures animals in powerful talons. Swallows small animals whole and regurgitates pellets of indigestible bones, hair or feathers. Is a vicious defender of nest, often striking intruders directly with talons. Flight is powerful and direct with stiff wing beats alternating with gliding.

CALLS

Most commonly heard call is a series of low, powerful hoots *hooo-hoo-hooooo-hoo-hoo*. The call, heard most frequently in late winter and early spring, carries a great distance and can be distinguished from the barred owl's by its lower and more consistent tone.

FOOD

Diet varies widely, but consists mostly of larger vertebrates such as rabbits and hares, as well as mice and voles. Also takes waterfowl and pheasants, and smaller passerine birds. Is known to eat fish, amphibians and lizards.

FAMILY LIFE
Monogamous pair; one of the earliest breeders among North American birds. Nests in abandoned tree nests of ravens, crows and hawks, and also in tree cavities, rock crevices, caves, in buildings, on ledges or in fallen hollow logs. Lines nest lightly with soft materials such as down and feathers. Re-uses nest year after year. The typical clutch of 2 to 3 eggs is incubated mostly by the female for 28 to 35 days. Semialtricial young remain in the nest for 35 to 45 days and are fed by both adults. One brood per year.

MIGRATION
Year-round resident.

CONSERVATION CONCERNS
Species status overall in North America is *secure* in the United States and Canada. Population increasing in Canada.

RELATED SPECIES
One of 18 species of owls belonging to the family *Strigidae* in North America. Is the only member of the genus *Bubo* in North America.

A great horned owl

BARRED OWL
(Strix varia)

The adult barred owl is a large,
deep-forest bird of prey with dark eyes.

The archetypal owl of deep forests, this efficient hunter has expanded its range northward and westward during the twentieth century to become one of the most widespread owls in North America.

APPEARANCE
Length: 21 inches. *Wingspan:* 42 inches. A fairly large brown owl with very dark eyes; pale light spots above heavy horizontal barring on throat and upper breast, and heavy dark vertical streaking on lighter underparts; round head with no ear tufts.

HABITAT
Lives in deep coniferous and mixed coniferous forests, wooded swamps and wetlands, bogs and riparian woods.

BEHAVIOR

Is nocturnal and crepuscular, but some-times active in the daytime. Has acute eyesight and hearing; hunts by sitting on a perch and waiting for prey to appear on the ground, then drops on silent wings to capture it. Is known to hunt this way for fish from a perch over water. Will also run along the ground and pounce on small animals. Plunges into the snow to capture rodents. Flight is buoyant and quiet on

The range of the barred owl

shallow flapping wings. Flaps and glides during longer flights. Is quite easy to approach when found roosting in the daytime.

CALLS

Song is a distinctive series of hoots, classically described as *who-cooks-for-you, who-cooks-for-you-aaalll?* with the last note drawn out. Calls include other hoots, barks and screams.

A curious barred owlet peers through the foliage of its nesting tree

FOOD
Diet consists of small mammals, invertebrates, birds, fish, reptiles and amphibians.

FAMILY LIFE
Monogamous pair; mates for life; nest is in a natural tree cavity that is located well above the ground; also occasionally utilizes the cavity atop a broken-off dead tree. The typical clutch of 2 or 3 eggs is incubated by the female for 28 to 33 days. Semialtricial young remain in the nest for 35 to 42 days and are fed by both parents. One brood per year.

MIGRATION
Year-round resident.

CONSERVATION CONCERNS
Species status overall in North America is *secure* in the United States and Canada. Population is possibly increasing in Canada. Is hybridizing with the endangered spotted owl of the Northwest and possibly pushing that species out of parts of its range.

RELATED SPECIES
Is 1 of 18 species of owls belonging to the family *Strigidae* in North America. Is a member of the genus *Strix*, which also includes the spotted and great gray owls.

NORTHERN HAWK OWL

(Surnia ulula)

A northern hawk in the Boreal forest

With its daytime hunting habits and sleek, goshawk-like appearance, this denizen of northern forests is the most un-owl-like of North America's owls.

APPEARANCE

Length: 16 inches. *Wingspan:* 28 inches. Is the size of a crow; face appears less flattened than other owls; bright yellow eyes; whitish facial disks framed by black with spotted white crown; upperparts are dark with white spotting; light underparts with fine horizontal barring; long pointed tail. Is often seen perching conspicuously on the very top of a conifer.

HABITAT

Is a boreal forest specialist found in conifers and mixed coniferous-deciduous woodlands, near northern bogs and muskeg, fens and swamps.

The range of the northern hawk owl

BEHAVIOR

Hunts during the daytime as well as at night. Selects high perch in the open to scan for prey and swoops down to fly fast and low over the ground as it approaches its quarry. Occasionally hovers before pouncing on prey. Is very tame and easy to approach. Hunts primarily by keen eyesight, but is often alerted to the presence of prey by sound. Is a fearless protector of the nest. Rarely walks on the ground. Flight is fast and hawk-like with rapidly beating wings alternating with short glides; is highly maneuverable as it passes through the trees.

CALLS

Alarm call is a rapid, repetitive series of notes *kee-kee-kee-kee*. Male utters rolling whistle *ululululu* during breeding season.

FOOD

Diet includes small mammals such as lemmings, mice, shrews and hares. Birds, particularly ground-dwelling species such as ptarmigan and grouse, are eaten more often in winter.

FAMILY LIFE

Monogamous pair; both the male and female participate in scraping out a cavity in a decaying tree, hollow stump or vacant woodpecker nest; occasionally may use cliff nest sites or abandoned stick nests of crows or hawks. Typical clutch of 3 to 9 eggs is incubated by the female for 25 to 30 days. Semialtricial young remain in the nest for 25 to 30 days and are fed by both parents.

MIGRATION
Nonmigratory, but may wander widely within its breeding range in search of food. Movement appears to be closely related to the population cycle and abundance of hares. Periodically irrupts southward in search of food when it is scarce in the North.

CONSERVATION CONCERNS
Species status overall in North America is *secure* in the United States and Canada.

RELATED SPECIES
Is 1 of 18 species of owls belonging to the family *Strigidae* in North America and the only member of its genus *Surnia*.

NORTHERN SAW-WHET OWL

(*Aegolius acadicus*)

The northern saw-whet owl is one of North
America's smallest species of owl

Though rarely observed, the call of this secretive little owl is often
heard at night in the mid-latitude woodlands it inhabits.

APPEARANCE
Length: 8 inches. *Wingspan:* 17 inches. The saw-whet is the second
smallest northern owl species after the northern pygmy owl, and
weighs about the same as an American robin. Large head with a
pale brown facial disk, a V-shaped white marking on face and large
yellow eyes, which give it the appearance of being ever-astonished;
no ear tufts; wide brown streaks and blotching on breast and belly;
upperparts are light brown with white spots on wings.

HABITAT

Inhabits moist evergreen and deciduous woodlands, as well as dense willow and alder thickets.

BEHAVIOR

Hunts at night from low perches, swooping to the ground to capture rodents and other small animals in its powerful talons. Its asymmetric ears allow it to hunt by sound alone when it becomes too dark to see. Usually forages along edges

The range of the northern saw-whet owl

or in forest openings. During the day it roosts in dense coniferous thickets, remaining all but invisible to humans. When one is discovered, however, the northern saw-whet can be quite tame, allowing a close approach. Flight is generally low to the ground and somewhat undulating on rapidly beating wings. Shows great skill at maneuvering through dense thickets.

CALLS

Is very vocal in the spring and early summer during the breeding season when the male sings an incessant *toot-toot-toot-toot*, at a rate of about 2 per second, sometimes for hours at a time. Also gives a hoarse *scree-aah, scree-aah, scree-ah*. At other times of the year, it is largely silent.

FOOD

Diet consists largely of rodents such as deer mice, voles, shrews, juvenile squirrels and chipmunks. Also occasionally takes small birds, bats and large invertebrates.

FAMILY LIFE

Monogamous pair; occasionally polygynous when prey is abundant; nests in tree cavities, especially abandoned flicker and pileated woodpecker holes, usually from 14–60 feet high; will also nest in artificial nesting boxes; no nest materials are used. Typical clutch of 5 or 6 eggs is incubated for 26 to 29 days by the female.

Semialtricial young remain in the nest for 27 to 34 days. Female feeds the young food that is given to her by the male for the first 18 days or so, then both parents feed the young during their remaining time in the nest. One brood per year.

MIGRATION
Generally a year-round resident, but some birds migrate south relatively short distances for the winter. Most of these birds arrive back on spring breeding grounds between late March and early May and head south again between September and November.

CONSERVATION CONCERNS
Species status overall is stable and *secure* for the United States and Canada. Its numbers are declining in parts of its range. Logging has reduced the amount of breeding habitat available, especially through the loss of appropriate dead trees (snags) for nesting.

RELATED SPECIES
Is 1 of 18 species belonging to the family *Strigidae* in North America. Closest relative is the boreal owl, which belongs to the same genus, *Aegolius*.

Did You Know?
Feathers are the one trait that distinguishes birds from any other group of animals. Other animals fly (bats), lay eggs (reptiles, amphibians, monotreme mammals) and have bills (duck-billed platypus), but only birds have feathers. They are used for flight, insulation, in sexual display, camouflage, sense of touch, to repel water and sound production. They often weigh more than a bird's skeleton. Preening, the daily maintenance of feathers, takes up much of a bird's waking hours and involves rearranging the delicate structures of the feathers, cleaning them and oiling them. Most birds have a preen gland on their rumps where they gather oil with the bill for distribution throughout the feathers. This oil helps keep the feathers flexible and waterproof, and inhibits the growth of harmful fungus and bacteria.

RUFFED GROUSE

(*Bonasa umbellus*)

A ruffed grouse struts through a woodland bog

The male's dramatic, low-frequency drumming of its wings on its breast is one of the hallmark springtime sounds heard in northern deciduous woodlands across North America.

APPEARANCE
Length: 17 inches. *Wingspan:* 22 inches. Is a rather chunky ground-dwelling bird; cryptic, mottled plumage with two distinct color morphs, gray and brown; upperparts either gray or brown or anything in between with heavy white spotting; gray color morph more common; underparts are lighter with heavy brown or gray barring; small head with a small crest and a chicken-like bill; multi-banded tail ends with a heavy dark bar.

A ruffed grouse at the edge of a dense forest

HABITAT

Lives in young deciduous and mixed deciduous-coniferous forests with dense understory of saplings and shrubs. Is found especially in woodlands dominated by aspen and poplar.

BEHAVIOR

Forages by browsing leaves and limbs of trees and shrubs for plant material such as aspen buds. Also picks food off the ground. Is very efficient at walking both on the ground and along branches in trees. Flight is explosive, low, direct and very short in a whirr of rapidly beating wings. Rarely flies farther than 600 feet. Repeated flushing can drive it to exhaustion.

CALLS

Utters a variety of peeps, hisses and chirping sounds, the most familiar being the *quit-quit-quit* sounds it makes when alerted to danger. To establish territory and attract females in spring, the male drums its wings against its breast faster and faster to produce a low thumping sound that carries a significant distance through the woods.

The range of the ruffed grouse

FOOD
Diet consists largely of aspen and other tree buds, flowers, leaves, seeds and berries. Insects and other invertebrates such as spiders and snails are also taken during summer.

FAMILY LIFE
Promiscuous; female builds a well-concealed ground nest in a deep depression near a tree trunk, or sheltered by a boulder, shrub or fallen log. The typically large clutch of 9 to 12 eggs is incubated by the female for 21 to 28 days. Precocial young leave the nest after only a few hours and are tended closely by the female for 10 to 12 days. The young are completely independent about 80 days later. One brood per year.

MIGRATION
Year-round resident.

CONSERVATION CONCERNS
Species status overall in North America is *secure* in the United States and Canada. Is a heavily hunted game species with over 3 million birds shot each year.

RELATED SPECIES
Is 1 of 12 species native to North America belonging to the family *Phasianidae*. The sole member of the genus *Bonasa*.

A conservation status map of the ruffed grouse

GAME BIRDS

NORTHERN BOBWHITE

(Colinus virginianus)

*A northern bobwhite male forages
in the grass at the edge of a woodland*

One of the most studied birds in the world, this little member of the
quail family, at home in open woodlands and fields, has had its
numbers decline significantly over recent decades.

APPEARANCE
Length: 10 inches. *Wingspan:* 13 inches. Is a small, chunky, short-
tailed and short-legged ground dweller; overall reddish-brown with
intricate scaling, striping and barring; males have a distinctive,
heavy white "eyebrow," a rufous cap and a white throat; the
female shares a similar pattern, but white is replaced by yellow-
brown; small, dark, chicken-like bill.

HABITAT

Inhabits open pine and mixed pine-hardwood forests, grown-over fields, smaller cultivated fields, natural grasslands and grass-brush rangelands.

BEHAVIOR

Forages by picking food from the ground and off low bushes, tree branches, shrubs and grass. Scratches at vegetation and leaf litter and pecks like a chicken. In snowy conditions, it

The range of the northern bobwhite

must find bare patches of ground to feed. Travels in small coveys of 8 to 15 birds during fall and winter. Is efficient at walking and running. The bird explodes from the ground quickly on whirring wings, then alternates rapid wing beats with gliding on stiffly held, downward-curving wings.

CALLS

Song is a clear whistling *bob-white, bob-white, bob-white* with the accent strongly on the second syllable. Also whistles *koy-kee*.

FOOD

Diet is largely plant-based and includes seeds, buds, berries, leaves and tubers. Also eats insects, spiders, snails and some small vertebrates.

FAMILY LIFE

Monogamous pair; both sexes participate in building a ground nest in a shallow depression, lined with grass and hidden by an arch of woven vegetation; nest has a small side entrance. The typical clutch of 14 to 16 eggs is incubated by both sexes for 23 to 24 days. Precocial young, fed by

A female northern bobwhite

both parents, are well devel-
oped at birth and leave the nest
shortly after hatching, achiev-
ing first flight after 12 to 14
days. One or more broods per
season.

MIGRATION
Year-round resident.

A conservation status map of the
northern bobwhite

CONSERVATION
CONCERNS
Species status overall in North America is *secure* in the United
States and *critically imperiled* in Canada. Species faces extirpation
in Ontario, the only part of its range in Canada. It may exist in
other parts of Canada, but those birds were introduced for game
hunting. Species has been declining across North America an average of 3.5 percent per year over the past few decades; despite this,
the species is still legally hunted in parts of the United States.

RELATED SPECIES
Is 1 of 6 species that belong to the family *Odontophoridae* (New
World quail) in North America and the only member of the genus
Colinus.

Did You Know?
Most woodland birds are virtually helpless when they hatch and
are born naked. They often have closed eyes and are largely
immobile. They require a lot of care and nurturing by parents
before they are able to leave the nest, but are less vulnerable to
predators than the young of birds such as bobwhites and grouse.
Their young are born with down and are almost immediately
mobile enough to follow parents around. Such birds that have
precocial young tend to have larger broods, since the chance of
losing some of them to predation is significantly greater. There are
also intermediate stages where young are born with varying
degrees of development.

WHITE-WINGED DOVE
(*Zenaida asiatica*)

The long, black cheek patch and white wing patches can be used to distinguish the white-winged dove from similar species

This gentle bird, like its sister species the mourning dove, is benefiting from human alteration of the landscape and is expanding its range in the southern part of the continent.

APPEARANCE

Length: 11.5 inches. *Wingspan:* 19 inches. Is similar in size and color to the mourning dove; overall light brown with conspicuous long white wing patches and dark primary feathers; dark mark below and behind eye; tail rounded and shorter than mourning dove's, with white rim around tail; orange eyes surrounded by a bright blue skin patch; blue bill.

HABITAT

Lives in dense, thorny woodlands and thickets along desert creeks and streams, suburban shade trees, parks, near water sources both natural and manmade. The planting of shade trees in residential areas and expanding agriculture have provided additional nesting and feeding habitats for the species. Tends to nest in the interior rather than at the edge of woodlands.

The range of the white-winged dove

BEHAVIOR

Forages on the ground by moving leaf litter with its bill. Spends more time feeding in trees and shrubs than the mourning dove. May travel great distances from breeding area to find food and water. Is gregarious and roosts in flocks, especially after breeding season. Flight is swift, quiet and more direct than the mourning dove. Walks in typical dove fashion with a bobbing head and short steps. Is fond of human water sources such as birdbaths and water tanks.

CALLS

The song is a cooing *two-looks-for you*, not unlike the call of a barred owl.

FOOD

Eats seeds, berries, fruits, acorns, agricultural grains such as sunflower seeds, safflowers and corn.

FAMILY LIFE

Monogamous pair; breeds in small colonies; both sexes participate (the male brings material, and the female builds) in building a flat nest of sticks, twigs, plant stems and grass in the fork of a shrub or a tree, or in a cactus; nest is occasionally placed on top of a deserted nest of another species. The typical clutch of 2 eggs is incubated by both the female and male for 13 to 14 days. Altricial young remain in the nest

A white-winged dove's blue eye-ring is apparent at close range

for 13 to 16 days and are fed "pigeon milk" (see mourning dove account) by both parents. Two or 3 broods per year.

MIGRATION
Most birds are year-round residents. Those that migrate arrive on breeding grounds from early April to late May. Fall migration generally occurs from late August to early October.

CONSERVATION CONCERNS
Species status overall in North America is *secure* in the United States. Is a hunted gamebird species in the western United States. Range is expanding northward. Adapts well to human alterations of the landscape, which may offset loss of natural habitat areas.

RELATED SPECIES
One of 9 native North American species that belong to the family of pigeons and doves, *Columbidae*. Its closest relative is the mourning dove, which is a member of the same genus *Zenaida*.

MOURNING DOVE

(*Zenaida macroura*)

*Though they nest in trees, mourning doves spend a
good deal of time on the ground*

Although not found in quite the astronomical numbers as was its
extinct cousin, the passenger pigeon, the mourning dove is nevertheless one of the most abundant and widespread birds in North
America.

APPEARANCE
Length: 12 inches. *Wingspan:* 18 inches. Is a slender bird with a
long, pointed, white-tipped tail and narrow wings; overall light
gray-brown with black spots on the rear part of wing; black spot
on lower cheek; the male has a slight pinkish tinge on upper breast
and neck.

HABITAT
Has a wide variety of habitats, including open woodlands, suburban, urban and agricultural areas with shade trees. Avoids heavily forested areas.

BEHAVIOR
Forages by gleaning food from the ground and from foliage. Is commonly seen at winter bird-feeding stations. Shows typical pigeon-like characteristic of jerking the head to look at something and pumping the head back and forth while walking. Drinks by sucking water rather than tilting head back to swallow. Flight is fast and direct with powerful wing beats. Wings whistle or squeak during takeoff. Is wary of humans due to centuries of hunting.

The range of the mourning dove

CALLS
The song is a mournful *oo-ah-oo-oo-oo*.

DOVES

An elegant bird, the mourning dove is fond of bird feeders in winter

FOOD
Diet consists almost exclusively of seeds. Also consumes waste grains.

FAMILY LIFE
Monogamous pair; is one of the most prolific breeders of all North American birds. The female builds a flat, flimsy nest of twigs and sticks that are gathered by the male; nest is lined with fine materials and placed in the fork of a branch, on the ground or other suitable surface; sometimes they will use the abandoned nest of a songbird. The typical clutch of 2 eggs is incubated by both sexes for 13 to 14 days. Altricial young remain in the nest for 12 to 14 days, during which time they are fed "pigeon's milk," a highly nutritious substance produced in the adult bird's crop. Two or 3 broods per year, but 5 or 6 broods per year in the South.

MIGRATION
Many birds are overwintering year-round residents. Those that migrate generally arrive on their breeding grounds during April and May. Fall migration usually occurs from mid-August to November.

CONSERVATION CONCERNS
Species status overall in North America is *secure* in the United States and Canada. Has benefited greatly from human alterations to the landscape since European settlement and has grown in population and range. The leading gamebird species with nearly *70 million* shot each year in those jurisdictions where it is legal to do so. It remains abundant second only to the red-winged blackbird in North America, but we must not forget the lesson taught by the extinction of its larger cousin, the passenger pigeon, once the world's most abundant bird, which was hunted into oblivion.

RELATED SPECIES
Is 1 of 9 native North American species that belong to the family of pigeons and doves, *Columbidae*. Its closest relative is the white-winged dove, which is a member of the same genus *Zenaida*.

RUBY-THROATED HUMMINGBIRD

(Archilochus colubris)

A male ruby-throated hummingbird hovering

This precious winged jewel of woodlands and gardens is the only species of hummingbird that breeds in eastern North America.

APPEARANCE

Length: 3.75 inches. *Wingspan:* 4.5 inches. Is tiny; both sexes have shimmering, green upperparts and whitish underparts, the male with green sides and flanks; the male has a black face and an iridescent red or "ruby" bib and throat patch that appears black in most light; female has a rounded tail with white outer feathers; male has dark green, forked tail; long, needle-like bill.

HABITAT

Inhabits deciduous or mixed deciduous-coniferous woodland, orchards and parks, as well as residential areas that are open with scattered trees and gardens.

BEHAVIOR

Forages primarily by hovering over flowers and inserting its bill to drink nectar. Also captures some insects and spiders. Is readily attracted to artificial feeders. The timing of the ruby-throated hummingbird's arrival in spring may depend on the previous arrival of yellow-bellied sapsuckers whose drilled sap wells provide a vital source of food prior to the availability of plant nectar later in spring. Is attracted to the color red. Flight is direct and bee-like with buzzing wings. Is masterful at hovering (including flying backwards) on invisibly fast "humming" wings.

The range of the ruby-throated hummingbird

CALLS

The loud hum of the wings is the sound heard most often. Calls are high, squeaking, chittering notes, sometimes in rapid succession. Also a soft *titip*.

FOOD

Diet is primarily the nectar of flowers. Also takes the sap running from yellow-bellied sapsuckers' drill holes, especially in the spring. Insects, spiders, and other small invertebrates are also eaten. Sugar-water mix is popular at feeders.

A male ruby-throated hummingbird shows off the feature for which it is named

FAMILY LIFE

Breeding season may coincide with the flowering of wild columbine in northern parts of its range. Female builds a tiny, knot-like, deeply cupped nest of plant thistles and plant down, buds, lichen and moss, held together with spider and cocoon silk and lined with soft plant down. Nest is usually placed toward the end of a downward-sloping branch which is sheltered from above, and sometimes located over water. The typical clutch of 2 eggs is incubated by the female for 11 to 16 days. Altricial young remain in the nest for 20 to 22 days and are fed by the female. One to 3 broods per year.

MIGRATION

Spring birds usually arrive on their breeding grounds between late April and late May and may depend on the earlier arrival of the yellow-bellied sapsucker (see "Behavior" section above). Fall migration generally occurs between early August and early October. This appears to coincide with the flowering of jewelweed and suggests that it is an important source of nectar that may influence the timing of its fall migration.

CONSERVATION CONCERNS

Species status overall in North America is *secure* in the United States and Canada. Evidence is mixed as to whether the population is increasing or declining.

RELATED SPECIES

Is 1 of 18 species of hummingbirds found in North America, all of which belong to the family *Trochilidae*. Closest relative is the black-chinned hummingbird, the only other member of the genus *Archilochus*.

A female ruby-throated hummingbird

RUFOUS HUMMINGBIRD

(Selasphorus rufus)

A male rufous hummingbird hovering

The most widespread of all the western North American humming-birds lives as far north as Alaska (the most northerly of any hummer) and is known for the tenacious defense of its nest from intruders.

APPEARANCE
Length: 3.75 inches. *Wingspan:* 4.5 inches. Male has a reddish-brown back (a small percentage of males have some green on the back), head and underparts; bright red throat; white breast patch; females have a green back and head, spotted throat and orange buff and white underparts.

HABITAT

Inhabits coniferous forests, mixed coniferous-deciduous woodlands, brushy areas, and thickets. It is found often adjacent to a meadow where there is a supply of flowers for nectar.

BEHAVIOR

Forages primarily by hovering to extract nectar from flowers. Is strongly attracted to red flowers. Also hawks for flying insects and hovers to pick spiders from webs. Drinks sap running from sapsucker drill holes. Prefers to feed early in the morning on flowers that may be exploited by other birds later in the day. In the extreme north of its range, it has the shortest season but the longest daylight period of any hummingbird for foraging. Flight is typical for a hummingbird with rapid direct flight on whirring wings and the ability to finely maneuver while hovering.

The range of the rufous hummingbird

CALLS

Call is a low-toned *chip chip chip* or a *tzee-chuppity-chuppity-chip*.

FOOD

Diet is primarily flower nectar, but also insects, spiders and other tiny invertebrates, and tree sap from sapsucker drill holes.

FAMILY LIFE

Polygamous; loosely semicolonial. The female builds a deeply cupped nest of moss, lichen, leaves, shredded bark, bud scales and plant fibers, held together by spider silk and lined with soft plant down. The nest is usually placed on a drooping lower limb of a coniferous tree, but a variety of off-ground sites are used, such as the fork of a shrub. It is often renovated and reused in subsequent years. Typical clutch of 2 eggs is incubated by the female for 12 to 14 days. Altricial young remain in the nest for 20 days and are fed by the female. One or 2 broods per year.

A male rufous hummingbird

MIGRATION

Spring birds arrive on their breeding grounds from early March to late April. Fall migration generally occurs from mid-July through August. Reaches the northernmost latitude (61 degrees) of any species of hummingbird and performs the longest migration of any bird on Earth relative to its body size.

CONSERVATION CONCERNS

Species status overall in North America is *secure* in the United States and Canada. Population is declining, but still common and widespread.

RELATED SPECIES

One of 18 species of hummingbirds found in North America, all of which belong to the family *Trochilidae*. Its closest 3 relatives are fellow members of the genus *Selasphorus*, which includes the broad-tailed, Allen's and calliope hummingbirds.

Did You Know?

Birds use several different methods for navigating over long distances and homing in on specific nesting sites. In general, 5 different techniques of navigation are used. On relatively clear days and clear moonlit nights, landmarks such as coastlines, rivers and mountain ranges are used by many bird species to find their way. When it's difficult or impossible to see the ground, birds that migrate at night rely on the position of the stars to navigate. To give one example of convincing evidence of this, a researcher showed indigo buntings a map of the night sky in a planetarium and found that the birds oriented themselves correctly using the "starry sky" projected above them. When he moved the position of the stars, the birds adjusted their orientation, too. Birds also use the position of the Sun relative to the Earth, smells and the Earth's magnetic field to find their way.

ACORN WOODPECKER

(Melanerpes formicivorus)

A female acorn woodpecker

This clown of western forests spends most of its time on the seemingly never-ending task of gathering acorns, which it hoards by the thousands.

APPEARANCE
Length: 9 inches. *Wingspan:* 17 inches. Black back and wings; bright red crown; conspicuous whitish eye; black sides of head; white patch on forehead that continues downward into a throat patch; black breast; white underparts with black streaks. The female has a black bar that separates the crown from the forehead.

HABITAT

Lives in primarily oak and mixed oak and pine woodlands. It requires lots of acorns and the appropriate dead trees to store them in; often lives in foothills.

BEHAVIOR

Forages socially in groups for acorns, which are stored individually in small pockets pecked in dead trees. Known as granaries, these trees are used year after year. Some granary trees hold as many as

The range of the acorn woodpecker

50,000 acorns. Other wooden structures, such as power poles, are also used. Will defend granaries from other woodpeckers and jays. Not all populations live in groups or store acorns. Also gleans

A male acorn woodpecker on an oak tree

insects and larvae from bark and captures insects in flight by hawking for them. Drills and drinks sap in the manner of sapsuckers. There is a strong social bond within groups. Is very noisy. Flight is undulating with rapid beating wings alternating with gliding.

CALLS
A raucous, hoarse *wicka-wicka-wicka*.

FOOD
Diet includes insects, acorns, seeds, fruit and berries. Acorns are most important in the fall and winter when insects are less available.

FAMILY LIFE
Cooperative breeders in groups of up to 16 birds, both sexes (plus members of the social groups) excavate a tree-hole nest from 6–60 feet above the ground and line it with wood chips. The typical clutch of 3 to 7 eggs is incubated for 11 to 14 days by both sexes as well as by other birds in the group. The altricial young remain in the nest for 30 to 32 days and are fed by both parents, plus helper birds. One or 2 broods per year.

MIGRATION
Year-round resident; one population in southeast Arizona migrates; other populations may wander in search of food from time to time.

CONSERVATION CONCERNS
Species status overall in North America is *secure* in the United States. Primary threats to populations are destruction of pine-oak habitat due to development and overgrazing of livestock.

RELATED SPECIES
Is 1 of 6 North American species that belong to the genus *Melanerpes*.

WOODPECKERS

GOLDEN-FRONTED WOODPECKER

(*Melanerpes aurifrons*)

A female golden-fronted woodpecker

This brash, noisy bird is a southern specialty, living only in Texas and Oklahoma where it is at the northern tip of its range.

APPEARANCE
Length: 9.5 inches. *Wingspan:* 17 inches. Back and wings have heavy, uniform white and black barring; rich, golden patch on nape and just above bill; the male has a red crown patch (lacking in the female); white rump and black tail; the side of the head, breast and belly are a pale brown, with a slight golden wash on the breast and belly (difficult to distinguish).

HABITAT

Lives in dry woodlands (especially mesquite), brushlands, riparian woods, parks and residential areas with sufficient trees.

BEHAVIOR

Forages low in trees where it gleans food from the surface or inserts its bill and probes with its long tongue to get at food beneath the bark. Feeds in open areas with short grass or bare ground, rarely beneath bushes or shrubs. Hawks for flying insect prey. Is sometimes found feeding on the ground in mixed flocks with mourning doves, flickers, meadowlarks

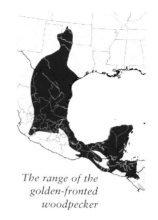

The range of the golden-fronted woodpecker

A golden-fronted woodpecker male

and other species. Hitches up vertical surfaces such as trunks, and hops on horizontal limbs and on the ground. Flight is undulating and swift with alternating flapping and gliding with wings held against its sides.

CALLS
Is noisy with a variety of harsh calls. Commonly heard are a grating *chick-ek* and a harsh *kurrr*.

FOOD
Diet includes a variety of insects and other invertebrates as well as acorns, pecans, mesquite beans, corn and citrus. Will take suet at feeders.

FAMILY LIFE
Monogamous pair; both sexes participate in excavating a cavity nest in a living or dead tree, usually 6 feet up or higher; will also nest in power poles, large posts and artificial nesting boxes; usually reuses previous nest. The typical clutch of 4 or 5 eggs is incubated by both sexes (the male at night and at times during the day) for 12 to 14 days. Altricial young remain in the nest for 30 days and are fed by both parents. One or 2 broods per year.

MIGRATION
Year-round resident.

CONSERVATION CONCERNS
Species status overall in North America is *secure* in the United States.

RELATED SPECIES
One of 6 North American species that belong to the genus *Melanerpes*. Is most closely related to the very similar red-bellied woodpecker with which it hybridizes.

DOWNY WOODPECKER

(Picoides pubescens)

A female downy woodpecker feeds on suet

This tame little woodpecker, one of the most commonly observed throughout much of North America, is a delight to watch as it crawls about the trunks of nearby trees or takes suet at the backyard feeder.

APPEARANCE

Length: 7 inches. *Wingspan:* 12 inches. Wings are black with white spots and barring; is named for the soft, downy white feathers in the middle of the large white patch on its back; underparts are white; white head and face with bold black stripe behind the eye, on the crown and on side of the throat; small, pointed bill; male has red patch at the back of the head; small dark spots or bars on outer tail feathers may help distinguish it from the very similar hairy woodpecker, but some populations of the larger birds possess these markings.

HABITAT

Inhabits deciduous and mixed deciduous-coniferous woodlands with plenty of open areas, riparian woodlands, orchards, urban woodlots, residential areas and parks with trees. Is a frequent visitor to bird feeders.

The range of the downy woodpecker

BEHAVIOR

Forages very actively by gleaning, probing and excavating its insect food from the bark of trees and also from tall, woody weeds. In many populations, the males tend to feed on smaller branches while the females feed on the trunks and larger branches. Will rarely hawk for flying insects. Drums on dead or hollow limbs and trunks. Usually hitches its way upward on tree surfaces. Flight is undulating with alternating rapid flapping and brief gliding with wings pulled against the body.

A female downy woodpecker

CALLS
Most commonly heard call is a soft, abrupt *pik*. Will also give a rattling, descending staccato call of the same note.

FOOD
Diet consists largely of insects, their larvae and eggs, spiders and other invertebrates, berries, seeds, sap from sapsucker holes and suet from bird feeders.

FAMILY LIFE
Monogamous pair; both sexes participate in excavating a tree-cavity nest, lined with wood chips and often camouflaged by moss or lichens surrounding the hole, placed in a dead limb (often part of a living tree) or in the trunk of a dead tree more than 10 feet above the ground. Will also nest in an artificial nesting box if it is of the proper dimensions. The typical clutch of 4 or 5 eggs is incubated by the male at night and the female during the day for a total of 12 days. Altricial young remain in the nest for 20 to 25 days and are fed by both parents. One brood per year.

MIGRATION
Year-round resident.

CONSERVATION CONCERNS
Species status overall for North America is *secure* for the United States and Canada.

A male downy woodpecker hitches down a tree while looking for insects

RELATED SPECIES
One of 9 species belonging to the genus *Picoides* in North America, including the Nuttall's, ladder-backed, American three-toed, black-backed, red-cockaded (an endangered species), white-headed and hairy woodpeckers. The hairy woodpecker is most similar in appearance and distribution.

HAIRY WOODPECKER

(Picoides villosus)

*A male hairy woodpecker
looking for insects*

One of the most widespread of all North American woodpeckers, the hairy woodpecker's color and size vary widely depending where on the continent it is found.

APPEARANCE
Length: 9.25 inches. *Wingspan:* 15 inches. Wings are black with white spots and barring, as if the bird is in dappled sunlight; is named for the lengthy filamentous feathers in the middle of the large white patch on its back; underparts are white; white head and face with bold black stripe behind the eye, on the crown and on the side of the throat; the male has a red patch at the back of the head; large, pointed bill; distinguishable from the very similar downy woodpecker by its larger bill and lack of dark bars or spots on the white tail feathers.

HABITAT

Inhabits deciduous, coniferous and mixed forests, as well as woodland swamps. Often moves from forests into more open environments such as treed residential areas and parks in winter.

BEHAVIOR

Forages by digging holes in trees with its chisel-like bill to reach insects using its long, barbed tongue. Is very adept at climbing up the trunks and large

The range of the hairy woodpecker

branches utilizing a typical woodpecker arrangement of 2 forward-facing toes and 2 facing back and a stiff tail for support. Is quite shy and inconspicuous during the breeding season, but is less fearful of humans when it visits bird feeders in the winter. Flight is quite undulating with alternating flapping and gliding with wings held against the body.

CALLS

The call is a loud, abrupt, metallic *peek*. Also utters a rapid progression of short, slurred notes that descends into a rattle.

FOOD

Diet consists primarily of wood-boring insects and other invertebrates. Also drinks sap from sapsucker holes. In winter it will feed on plant-based food such as beechnuts and acorns.

FAMILY LIFE

Monogamous pair; both sexes participate in excavating a nest hole in a tree and lining it with wood chips; nest placed just above ground up to over 50 feet high. The typical clutch of 3 to 6 eggs is incubated by both sexes (the male incubates during the night) for 11 to 15 days. Altricial young remain in the nest for 28 to 30 days and are fed by both parents. One brood per year unless the first brood fails.

MIGRATION
Is generally a year-round resident, although some northern populations may wander in winter to find food.

CONSERVATION CONCERNS
Species status overall in North America is *secure* in the United States and Canada. Is common within its large range, although some declines in populations may be caused by forest fragmentation.

RELATED SPECIES
Is 1 of 9 species belonging to the genus *Picoides* in North America. The downy woodpecker is most similar in appearance and distribution.

YELLOW-BELLIED SAPSUCKER

(*Sphryapicus varius*)

A yellow-bellied sapsucker searches for a suitable place to drill a sap hole in a birch tree

Famous for its rather comical name, this small woodpecker is the widest ranging of the 4 species of sapsuckers in North America.

APPEARANCE
Length: 8.5 inches. *Wingspan:* 16 inches. Back is black with copious messy white markings; wings are black with a long, narrow white patch; bright red crown adjacent to a black patch on the back of the head; black-and-white face with a long white mustache; a red throat on the male and white on the female; underparts are yellowish-white with dark chevrons down the sides and flanks; long, stiff tail.

HABITAT
Lives in mixed deciduous-coniferous forest and other woodlands with small open spaces; often near water.

BEHAVIOR
Forages by drilling shallow holes (often neatly aligned horizontally) in the bark of trees. It first consumes the nutritious inner bark and later returns to drink the sap that oozes from the holes. Creates a network of sap wells and maintains

The range of the yellow-bellied sapsucker

them to ensure a continuous supply of food. Hawks for insects as well as picking those that are attracted to the sap. Will sometimes dip captured insects in the sap. Sapsuckers are known to take sap from nearly 250 native species of trees. Guards drilled trees that are actively oozing from other birds and mammals, including hummingbirds. Despite this, hummingbirds have a close relationship with sapsuckers, often placing their nests near sap wells to take advantage of the nutritious food they provide. Sapsuckers also cache food. Flight is undulating with alternating rapid flapping and gliding.

CALLS
Is often silent, but its most frequently heard call is a nasal, descending *mee-yew* almost cat-like in character. Also heard is a *kee-err, kee-err*, given when the bird is alarmed. The male performs a staccato drumming.

FOOD
Diet is quite varied and includes tree sap, insects (especially ants), other invertebrates, berries, nuts, acorns and bark cambium (inner bark). Will take suet at winter feeders and will drink nectar from hummingbird feeders.

FAMILY LIFE

Monogamous pair; both sexes participate in excavating a cavity nest that is lined with wood chips. Nests are usually placed in living trees, but also in dead ones, frequently located near water. Often returns to the same tree (but not necessarily the same hole) year after year. Deserted sapsucker holes play a vital role in the ecology of the northern flying squirrel, which uses them to nest in. The typical clutch of 5 or 6 eggs is incubated by the male at night and the female during the day for a total of 12 or 13 days. Altricial young remain in the nest for 25 to 29 days and are fed sap and insects by both parents. One brood per year.

MIGRATION

Normally arrives on its spring breeding grounds between late March and early May. Fall migration generally occurs between early September and late October.

CONSERVATION CONCERNS

Species status overall in North America is *secure* in the United States and Canada. Some surveys suggest the population may be declining. In the southern Appalachians and in southern Ontario it is listed as a "species of concern."

A conservation status map of the yellow-bellied sapsucker

RELATED SPECIES

Is 1 of 4 species of sapsuckers in North America, all belonging to the genus *Sphyrapicus*.

NORTHERN FLICKER

(Colaptes auratus)

The red-shafted race of the northern flicker

The French name for the northern flicker, *Pic Flamboyant*, says it all: This is a noisy, animated, brightly colored, flamboyant bird, North America's ground-loving woodpecker.

APPEARANCE

Length: 12.5 inches. *Wingspan:* 20 inches. Two races exist: the red-shafted western bird and the yellow-shafted of the East and North. A large, overall brown woodpecker; the back is gray-brown with conspicuous black barring; crown and back of neck is gray; under-parts are light brown and heavily spotted with black; large black, crescent-shaped bib; long, stiff tail; long bill. The yellow-shafted male has a bright red crescent on the back of the head, and a black mustache (the female lacks the mustache). Both sexes of this race have yellow feather shafts in their wings. The red-shafted male has a gray face and throat, a red mustache and lacks the red crescent on the neck (the female lacks the mustache). Both sexes of this race have red feather shafts in their wings.

HABITAT
Lives in practically any woodland habitat that is reasonably open. Is also found on or near farmlands, residential areas, orchards and parks as long as trees are present or near and there is open ground for feeding.

The range of the northern flicker

BEHAVIOR
Forages primarily on the ground where it chisels then probes into the soil to pick insects. Regularly feeds at anthills where it uses its extremely long tongue (will extend nearly 2 inches past the tip of the bill) to pull ants out of the ground. Also gleans food from bark and foliage and will occasionally hawk for flying insects. Hops on the ground, and rarely walks or runs. Flight is typical undulating "flap-bounding" flight of woodpeckers where flapping is alternated with pulling wings to the side.

CALLS
Has many loud distinctive calls. Most commonly heard is the repetitive *wicker, wicker, wicker* call. Also utters a loud, piercing *cleer*.

FOOD
Eats more ants than any other North American bird. One specimen of a flicker was found to have 3,000 ants in its stomach. Also eats beetles and other insects. Fruit, seeds, nuts, acorns and berries are also taken, especially in winter when animal-based food is scarce. The red-shafted race eats more insect food in winter than the yellow-shafted race.

FAMILY LIFE

Monogamous pair; both male and female participate in excavating the nest in a dead tree or large branch up to 90 feet above the ground. Will also excavate in power poles, the sides of buildings, nest boxes and even in dirt banks (occasionally evicting a kingfisher or a bank swallow). May return to the nest year after year. The typical clutch of 5 to 8 eggs is incubated by both sexes for 11 to 16 days. Altricial young remain in the nest for 25 to 28 days and are fed by both parents. One brood (occasionally 2 in the South).

MIGRATION

Is a year-round resident throughout much of its range. Those that migrate (more northerly breeding birds) usually arrive on their breeding grounds between mid-March and late April. Fall migration generally occurs from early September to early November.

The yellow-shafted race of the northern flicker

CONSERVATION CONCERNS

Species status overall in North America is *secure* in the United States and in Canada. Common and widespread though it is, the flicker is declining throughout the continent, especially in the East. Habitat destruction, as well as the removal of dead trees and limbs from residential areas and parks, is decreasing the number of nesting sites available.

RELATED SPECIES

The northern flicker is broken down into 2 distinct forms, the yellow-shafted flicker of the East and North, and the red-shafted form of the West. The very similar gilded flicker, once thought a race of the northern flicker, has recently been given separate status as a species. All flickers belong to the genus *Colaptes*.

PILEATED WOODPECKER

(Dryocopus pileatus)

*A male pileated woodpecker hitching its way
up the trunk of a tree*

The sight of this impressive bird maneuvering deftly on the wing beneath the canopy of the forest is something not soon forgotten.

APPEARANCE

Length: 16.5 inches. *Wingspan:* 29 inches. Very large crow-sized woodpecker with a long neck; mostly black with a white wing patch on top and a large white area on underside of the wings that is visible in flight; large white head with a prominent scarlet crest, a bold black eye-line and a long chisel-like bill; male possesses a scarlet mustache and forehead that distinguish it from the female; broad white chin patch.

HABITAT

Lives in large tracts of old-growth or mature coniferous, deciduous and mixed forests or younger forests with high crown canopies and scattered large, dead trees for nesting and foraging. Also wooded residential areas, and parkland with large trees. Only large-diameter trees are thick enough to provide the space needed for a nest.

The range of the pileated woodpecker

BEHAVIOR

Forages by powerfully chiselling into large living or dead trees then using its long, barbed tongue to get at insects. Will also strip bark from trees. Rectangular feeding holes can be up to a foot long and 8 inches deep which can result in the tree eventually breaking. Also pecks at fallen logs, gleans insects from branches and digs in the ground to find food. If naturally hollow trees aren't available, it will excavate cavities to roost in. Its excavations are an important factor in the ecology of forests as they provide shelter and nesting places for a variety of other birds, as well as mammals, reptiles, amphibians and invertebrates. Moves efficiently on tree trunks by gripping with powerful toes and supporting itself with its stiff tail. Flight is direct with powerful wing beats alternating with wings folded at sides; over a distance it appears undulating.

CALLS

A commonly heard call is a repetitive rising and falling series of notes, *cuk-cuk-cuk-cuk*, similar to the northern flicker, but lower pitched and louder. Pairs also communicate by performing various other calls. In addition to vocal calls, it will perform a rolling, resonant drumming by pounding on a tree.

FOOD

Diet consists of carpenter ants, wood-boring beetle larvae and other invertebrates that may be found beneath bark and in rotting wood, as well as fruits, acorns, beechnuts, conifer seeds and sap.

FAMILY LIFE

Monogamous pair; will defend territory year-round; the male and female excavate a large cavity high up in a mature tree to be used as a nest, which may be lined by wood chips. The typical clutch of 4 eggs is incubated by both the male (who incubates at night) and the female for 15 to 18 days. The altricial young remain in the nest for 26 to 28 days and are fed by both sexes. One brood per year.

MIGRATION

Year-round resident.

CONSERVATION CONCERNS

Species status overall in North America is *secure* in the United States and Canada. Population has increased in recent decades. However, the population size is limited by the amount of suitable mature forest habitat available. Unfortunately, such older growth woodlands are also important for the timber industry and their continued destruction can spell nothing but trouble for the pileated woodpecker if such habitat is not protected. Illegal shooting continues to be a problem for the species.

RELATED SPECIES

In North America, only the ivory-billed woodpecker, which may or may not still exist, resembles the pileated in size, shape and character.

EASTERN WOOD-PEWEE

(Contopus virens)

An eastern wood-pewee singing in the spring

The loud, distinctive song of this inconspicuous little flycatcher ensures that it will be heard before it is seen.

APPEARANCE
Length: 6.25 inches. *Wingspan:* 10 inches. Is distinguished reliably from the virtually identical western wood-pewee by voice. Dull grayish, olive upperparts with the head appearing darker; faint white eye-ring; yellow lower mandible and black upper mandible; wings are quite dark with distinct white wingbars; breast and belly are a dusky olive or gray, somewhat lighter than the back; black feet and legs.

HABITAT

Inhabits a wide variety of wooded landscapes that contain large trees. Is found in deciduous, coniferous and mixed forest, forest edges, woodlots, roadsides, thick shrubs, old orchards, residential shade trees, open pine woods (in southern parts of its range) and riverside habitats on the plains. Is generally found from mid-level to high up in the canopy.

The range of the eastern wood-pewee

BEHAVIOR

Forages by making hawking flights for flying insects from a favorite perch located among the trees. Will return time after time to the same perch after sallying for prey. Turns its head from side to side as it scans for insects. Will occasionally hover for insects as well as glean them from foliage. Vigorously defends its nesting territory by attacking larger birds. Flight is direct with shallow wing beats.

CALLS

Song is a long, slurred whistle *pee-you-wee*, with the second note lower and the last note rising. After a few repeats this phrase is followed by a *pee-year* with the second note falling in pitch. The common call is a short *chip*.

FOOD

Eats insects in flight almost exclusively, including bees, wasps, flies and moths. Occasionally takes spiders, as well as berries.

FAMILY LIFE
Monogamous pair; the female builds a shallow, cup-shaped nest of grass, weed stems, bark, cocoons, plant fibers and grass, covered in a layer of lichens for camouflage and placed either in the fork of a branch or saddling a branch quite high up in a tree. The cryptic nature of the nest has made this aspect of the eastern wood-pewee's biology difficult to study. The typical clutch of 2 to 4 eggs is incubated by the female for 12 to 13 days. The altricial young remain in the nest for 14 to 18 days and are fed by both parents. One brood per year.

MIGRATION
Is one of the latest of the spring migrants, generally arriving on its breeding grounds in early to mid-May. Fall migration generally occurs between mid-August and mid-October.

CONSERVATION CONCERNS
Species status overall in North America is *secure* in the United States and Canada. However, declines have been noted throughout the continent, particularly in Canada. The species seems to be sensitive to the destruction of understory habitat caused by the browsing of abundant white-tailed deer. Population is also affected by loss of wintering habitat in South America.

RELATED SPECIES
Is a member of the large *Tyrannidae* family, which includes all the flycatchers of North America. Its closest relatives are the western wood-pewee, olive-sided flycatcher, greater pewee and northern beardless tyrannulet, all of which belong to the genus *Contopus*.

BLACK PHOEBE

(Sayornis nigricans)

*On a typical perch over a streambed, a black phoebe
awaits an opportunity to swoop on prey*

The energetic, water-loving black phoebe is the only small black-
and-white flycatcher in North America.

APPEARANCE

Length: 7 inches. *Wingspan:* 11 inches. Upperparts are dark-
charcoal gray; the head is almost black; white belly; long tail is
constantly pumping up and down; bill is medium length, somewhat
flattened in cross section, with bristles around the mouth opening.

HABITAT

Inhabits woodlands, farmlands with scattered trees, coastal cliffs and even suburbs, all in close proximity to water. Prefers riparian woodlands. A nearby source of mud is necessary for nest building. The growing number of artificial ponds and waterways in its western habitat has resulted in a growing population.

The range of the black phoebe

BEHAVIOR

In typical flycatcher fashion, the black phoebe is very active and adroit in the air. It forages by swooping from low, often shaded perches to capture insects in midair over the water, using spring-like ligaments to snap its bill shut on prey. Often will sally for insects from boulders located in streams, and occasionally will capture small fish near the surface. In winter will glean insects directly from the ground. Regurgitates pellets full of indigestible insect parts in the manner of an owl. Flight is buoyant on rapidly beating wings.

Common in its range, the black phoebe is the only very dark flycatcher species in the West

CALLS

The song is a series of high-pitched, shrill whistles *pee-weer, pee-weer*, repeated both while perched and in flight. The call is a clear *chip*.

FOOD

Diet consists almost entirely of insects, particularly aquatic ones such as mayflies. Small minnows are also taken. On rare occasions it will eat small berries.

FAMILY LIFE

Monogamous pair; the female builds a nest of mud-pellets lined with plant fibers, hair, grass and rootlets, which is usually placed over water and adhered to a vertical surface such as a rock face, boulder, bridge or other solid structure; will often refurbish an older nest. The typical clutch of 4 eggs is incubated by the female for 15 to 17 days. Altricial young remain in the nest for 14 to 21 days and are fed by both parents. Two or 3 broods per year.

MIGRATION

Generally a year-round resident throughout its range.

CONSERVATION CONCERNS

Species status overall in North America is *secure* in the United States with the population possibly increasing.

RELATED SPECIES

It is 1 of 3 species of phoebes in North America, all belonging to the genus *Sayornis*. The other 2 are Say's phoebe and the eastern phoebe.

A conservation status map of the black phoebe

VERMILION FLYCATCHER

(Pyrocephalus rubinus)

The male vermilion flycatcher's bold plumage is unmistakable

Few species in North America can match the spectacular beauty of this denizen of streamside woods in the arid southwestern United States.

APPEARANCE

Length: 6 inches. *Wingspan:* 10 inches. The only red North American flycatcher, the male is a brilliant red overall with black wings, back and mask; the female is mostly gray with white underparts streaked in gray; white throat; belly has a wash of pink or salmon.

HABITAT

Lives in riparian woodlands of cotton-wood, willow and mesquite as well as brushy areas along streams, rivers, creeks, ponds and human-made canals and waterways. Less commonly inhabits open woodland of oak and juniper.

The range of the vermilion flycatcher

BEHAVIOR

Sits and waits on a low exposed perch such as a weed or a shrub, sometimes over water, then hawks insects by sallying forth to capture them on the wing or on the ground. Will often hover. Pumps and spreads its tail while perched. Is somewhat tame and approachable. Will regurgitate indigestible insect parts. Normal flight is typical of many small flycatchers, with a shallow, fast fluttering of the wings. Also performs a spectacular courtship flight high above the trees where it flutters through the air while singing.

CALLS

The song, sung in flight by the male during courtship, is a series of high-pitched, soft, twittering *pit-i-tsee, pit-i-tsee*, rising and falling and ending in a trill. Call is a high *peet*.

FOOD

Diet is made up of almost exclusively insects including a large proportion of bees.

FAMILY LIFE

Monogamous pair; the female builds a loosely made cup-shaped nest of twigs, grass, rootlets, weeds and feathers that is often held together by spider silk and is usually placed in the horizontal fork of a tree from just above ground level to 60 feet up. The typical clutch of 3 eggs is incubated by the female for 14 to 15 days. Altricial young remain in the nest for 14 to 16 days and are fed by both parents. Two broods per year.

The more subdued color of the female vermilion flycatcher has a subtle beauty

MIGRATION
Year-round resident.

CONSERVATION CONCERNS
Species status overall in North America is *secure* in the United States, but declining due to the destruction of breeding habitat in riparian areas.

RELATED SPECIES
One of 33 regularly occurring members of the family *Tyrannidae* in North America. The only member of the genus *Pyrocephalus*, the vermilion flycatcher most closely resembles the three phoebes of the genus *Sayornis*.

A conservation status map of the vermilion flycatcher

GREAT CRESTED FLYCATCHER

(Myiarchus crinitus)

A great-crested flycatcher perched and ready to swoop for flying insects

More often heard than seen, the great crested flycatcher spends much of its time high among the foliage of the forest canopy, from whence its loud song resonates through the trees.

APPEARANCE

Length: 8.75 inches. *Wingspan:* 13 inches. Is a large, sleek, almost robin-sized flycatcher; upperparts are olive-gray with some black on wings; white wingbars; bright cinnamon color on wings and tail is unmistakable; crest on the head (not always visible), long black bill and long tail; gray throat and upper breast and yellow belly. Because of its distinctiveness, it is one of the easiest flycatcher species to identify.

HABITAT

Inhabits deciduous forest edges, open mature woodland, wooded parks, orchards and openings in dense second growth. Availability of nesting cavities is essential to its presence.

The range of the great crested flycatcher

BEHAVIOR

Hawks flying insects by sallying forth from a perch. Also gleans food from foliage, as well as hovering and then capturing prey. Usually hunts higher in the forest than other flycatchers, often in the canopy. The male vigorously defends the nesting territory from other males of the species, often fighting with them aggressively in midair, and occasionally pulling out one another's feathers in the process. Both male and female will attack larger birds such as crows or hawks that enter the vicinity of the nest. Flight is direct and buoyant.

CALLS

Dawn and twilight song is an alternating, repeated *wee-reep, wee-ah*. Most common call is a loud, clear whistled *queep*, sometimes followed by a rolling *purreet*.

FOOD

Eats larger insects such as beetles, caterpillars, moths, katydids, crickets. Also consumes fruit and berries. Occasionally will eat vertebrates such as small lizards.

FAMILY LIFE

Monogamous pair; the only cavity-nesting flycatcher in eastern North America. Both male and female prepare a nest in an abandoned woodpecker hole, natural tree hole or a nesting box. The nest is lined and filled with various materials such as bark, grass, twigs and feathers, and is usually located very close to the opening. The nest is often completed by placing a recently shed snakeskin inside. The typical clutch of 4 to 6 eggs is incubated by the female for 13 to 15 days. Altricial young remain in the nest for 13 to 15 days and are fed by both parents. One brood per year.

MIGRATION
Spring birds generally arrive on their breeding ground between mid-April and mid-May. Fall migration generally occurs from late August to late September.

CONSERVATION CONCERNS
Species status overall in North America is *secure* in the United States and Canada. This species may be benefiting from increased forest fragmentation that results in more suitable habitat.

RELATED SPECIES
Is 1 of 4 larger flycatcher species in North America that belong to the genus *Myiarchus*.

ALDER FLYCATCHER

(*Empidonax alnorum*)

An alder flycatcher perched and waiting for prey

This drab flycatcher of wet thickets is more often heard than seen.

APPEARANCE

Length: 5.75 inches. *Wingspan:* 8.5 inches. A small sparrow-sized bird with an overall dull olive-gray back and a lighter belly; dark gray wings show two distinct white horizontal bars; long tail; large head; distinctive white ring around the eye; a long, broad bill that is black on the top and pale orange underneath; white throat and chin. The sexes are alike and are virtually identical in appearance to the willow flycatcher.

HABITAT

Generally inhabits alder and willow thickets around swamps, damp woodlands, streams, freshwater marshes, fens and bogs.

BEHAVIOR

Although shy and difficult to see, the alder flycatcher is an extremely active bird that forages by sallying forth to capture insects in midair before immediately returning to its perch. Hunts

The range of the alder flycatcher

mostly in the alder thickets and low brush surrounding a wet meadow or swamp. Flycatchers in general have somewhat long wings for their size, giving them incredible agility and quickness in the air. Flight is direct with shallow fluttering in typical flycatcher fashion.

CALLS

Is virtually silent except during breeding season. The male alder flycatcher's song is a wheezing *ree-bee-o*. Its song is the only way to positively distinguish it from the very closely related willow flycatcher whose song is a slurred *fitz-bew*. The 2 species are so similar that until quite recently they were considered the same species, the Traill's flycatcher. Calls of the alder flycatcher include a simple *pit* and *zee-oo*.

FOOD

Diet is primarily flying insects, but also includes crawling insects, spiders and other invertebrates. Berries and seeds are also sometimes consumed.

FAMILY LIFE

Monogamous pair; the untidy, cup-shaped nest is placed in the crotch of a bush or small tree. It is made of grass, plant stems, bark and other fibers and lined with fine grasses, plant down and pine needles. The typical clutch of 3 or 4 eggs is incubated by the female for 12 to 14 days. The altricial young stay in the nest for 13 days and are fed by both parents. One brood per year.

MIGRATION

Generally arrives on its breeding grounds in May or June, and departs on its southerly migration during August and September.

CONSERVATION CONCERNS

Species status overall in North America is *secure* in the United States and Canada. Population may be increasing, and is relatively common within its range.

RELATED SPECIES

Is 1 of 11 species of flycatchers in the genus *Empidonax*, and virtually identical in appearance and behavior to the willow flycatcher.

WILLOW FLYCATCHER

(Empidonax traillii)

Willow flycatchers hunt by waiting on a perch and then hawking for flying insects

So similar in appearance are the willow and alder flycatchers that until 1973 they were both considered the same species, the Traill's flycatcher.

APPEARANCE

Length: 5.75 inches. *Wingspan:* 8.5 inches. Is a small sparrow-sized bird with an overall dull gray back and a lighter belly; very slightly longer bill and more rounded wings than the alder flycatcher; dark gray wings show two distinctly white horizontal bars; long tail; large head; thin white ring around the eye; a long, broad bill that is black on the top and pale orange underneath; white throat and chin. Northern birds tend to have darker heads, while birds of the southwest desert areas are lighter. Sexes look alike. Most flycatchers in the *Empidonax* genus are very similar and are difficult to tell apart by sight alone.

HABITAT
Prefers shrubby, damp habitats such as willow thickets. The *extimus* race of the Willow flycatcher of the southwestern United States is found almost exclusively in river and streamside woods.

The range of the willow flycatcher

BEHAVIOR
This very shy bird forages by sallying forth from a conspicuous perch to capture insect prey in flight. Will also glean insects as it hovers and will occasionally take prey directly from the ground. Flight is direct with shallow fluttering in typical flycatcher fashion.

CALLS
Song is an abrupt *fitz-bew* with the accent on the first syllable. Call is a simple *whit*.

The songs of the willow and alder flycatchers are innate (completely instinctive) and don't have to be learned like other songbirds.

FOOD
Diet includes flying insects, as well as insects, larvae and other invertebrates that are found on foliage or on the ground. Berries are also taken.

FAMILY LIFE
Monogamous pair; the female builds a loosely woven cup-shaped nest of weed stems, bark and grasses, lined with fine grass and placed in the fork of a deciduous tree or shrub. The typical clutch of 3 or 4 eggs is incubated for 12 to 15 days by the female. Altricial young remain in the nest for 13 to 14 days and are fed by both parents. One brood per year.

MIGRATION
Late migrants with a short breeding season, birds generally arrive on their breeding ground from early May to early June. Fall migration occurs from mid-August to mid-September.

CONSERVATION CONCERNS
Species status overall in North America is *secure* in the United States and Canada, but significantly declining in Pacific U.S. states and British Columbia. The species is also vulnerable in Atlantic Canada due to its historically low numbers there.

The *extimus* subspecies of the southwestern United States is listed as an *endangered*. Destruction of its shrubby riparian habitat by livestock grazing, water diversions, flooding, development and recreation is blamed for its perilous situation.

A conservation status map of the willow flycatcher

RELATED SPECIES
One of 11 quite similar flycatchers in North America, all of which belong to the genus *Empidonax*. Most closely resembles the alder flycatcher, which until recently was considered to be the same species.

DUSKY FLYCATCHER

(Empidonax oberholseri)

A dusky flycatcher

Quite common throughout its range, this small, inconspicuous bird is often confused with the Hammond's flycatcher and gray flycatcher, which it closely resembles.

APPEARANCE

Length: 5.75 inches. *Wingspan:* 8.25 inches. Overall olive-gray; wings have white wingbars and are slightly darker than the rest of the body; underparts are light gray to whitish with a slight olive green wash on breast and belly; lighter overall than most species of flycatchers; short bill and a long tail.

HABITAT
Lives in open coniferous and mixed woodlands, aspen groves, streamside willow thickets, mountain scrubland and open brushy areas.

BEHAVIOR
Primarily an aerial feeder, it forages from a perch located fairly low in vegetation by hawking for prey in midair. Occasionally will pounce on insects or other small invertebrate prey on the ground or glean them from foliage.

The range of the dusky flycatcher

Often flicks its tail upward while perched and occasionally flicks its wings. Flight is typically flycatcher-like with a rapid, shallow fluttering.

CALLS
The song is a simple melody of three phrases *shir-ip*, *breep* and a clear *sweet*. Call is a soft *whit* and the male utters a 2-tone *doo-widee*.

FOOD
Diet consists of insects exclusively, particularly moths and other flying species.

FAMILY LIFE
Monogamous pair; the female builds a cup-shaped nest of woven plant fibers, animal hair, grasses and bark relatively close to the ground in the low crotch of deciduous shrubs or trees. The typical clutch of 3 to 4 eggs is incubated by the female for 12 to 16 days. Altricial young remain in the nest for about 18 days and are fed by both parents. One brood per year.

MIGRATION
Migratory, but relatively little is known about the timing of its travels.

A dusky flycatcher showing its olive green back

CONSERVATION CONCERNS

Species status overall in North America is *secure* in the United States and Canada. Populations are possibly increasing, but it is difficult to tell due to the potential confusion of this flycatcher with the extremely similar Hammond's and gray flycatchers. Dusky flycatchers are vulnerable to severe weather such as prolonged rains or unseasonable snows, which can wipe out an entire local breeding population. As is the case with many species of woodland birds, especially in the West where water supplies for humans can be at a premium, the dusky flycatcher is susceptible to streamside habitat loss caused by water diversions, flood control, urbanization and grazing.

RELATED SPECIES

One of the 11 small North American flycatchers, all belonging to the genus *Empidonax*.

AMERICAN ROBIN

(Turdus migratorius)

A male American robin in spring

This most familiar of North American birds is the largest member of the thrush family and possibly the most abundant bird on the continent.

APPEARANCE

Length: 10 inches. *Wingspan:* 15 inches. Is a large songbird; dark gray upperparts and head; fairly thin yellow bill; and a broken white eye-ring. The male's chest is a deep brick red, and the female's is usually a little duller. Both sexes have a white lower belly and white outer tips on the end of the tail.

HABITAT

Is a habitat generalist found in most forests, open woodlands, riparian woods, cut-over areas, parklands, gardens, lawns and agricultural areas. Can be found in the deepest wilderness areas or in distinctly urban settings where trees are found.

The range of the American robin

BEHAVIOR

Forages in its familiar way by running across open grassy areas, then stopping and taking prey such as earthworms. Also gleans food from among vegetation and the branches of trees and shrubs. Is usually solitary or in pairs during the breeding season, but assembles into flocks (sometimes massive in size) during migration. Is quite tame. Hops, walks or runs on the ground. Flight is fast and direct on quickly beating wings.

CALLS

Song is a rich, bubbling, fluted series of phrases, *cheery-up*, *cheerry-do*, *cheery-up*, *cherey-dee*, usually sung before dawn and again late in the evening. Calls are a piercing *sileet* and a soft *too-too-too*.

FOOD

Diet includes insects, earthworms, grubs and other invertebrates such as snails. Berries and fruit are also taken, especially in winter when insects aren't available.

FAMILY LIFE

Monogamous pair; occasionally will nest in loose colonies. Both sexes (mostly the female) participate in building a cup-shaped nest of a loosely woven foundation of grasses and twigs with a dried mud cup lined with fine grass that is placed in trees under the shelter of foliage, in buildings or on natural ledges suitable for supporting the nest. The typical clutch of 4 eggs is incubated by the female for 12 to 14 days. Altricial young remain in the nest for 14 to 16 days and are fed mostly by the female. The male will tend the young while the female incubates a second clutch. One to 3 broods per year.

MIGRATION
Robins within the continental United States are generally year-round residents. Populations in Canada are mostly migratory. Birds that migrate usually arrive on their breeding grounds between March and April. Fall migration generally occurs between late August and November.

CONSERVATION CONCERNS
Species status overall in North America is *secure* in the United States and Canada.

RELATED SPECIES
One of 18 breeding species or regular visitors that belongs to the family *Turdidae* in North America. The only other species in the genus *Turdus* that breeds here is the rare clay-colored robin.

Did You Know?
The great majority of bird species (about 90 percent) are monogamous and form a common pair bond with only 1 member of the opposite sex. The reason monogamy is so popular is because having both parents involved in rearing the young is generally more successful than having just one parent. How long a particular bird remains bonded to its partner depends on the species. Most woodland birds will remain with the same mate for one breeding

An American robin on a frosty winter day

season, while others, such as the American robin and mourning dove, may stay with the same mate for several seasons. Eagles and some owls, such as the barred owl, mate for life.

HERMIT THRUSH
(*Catharus guttatus*)

When alarmed the hermit thrush weakly flutters its wings

Despite its drab appearance, there are few species that can match the beauty of the hermit thrush's ethereal, flute-like song.

APPEARANCE

Length: 6.75 inches. *Wingspan:* 11.5 inches. Is smaller than a robin; upperparts are olive brown to reddish brown, depending on where it is found within its continent-wide range; grayish-white breast and belly with bold brown spots on the upper breast and throat; thin white eye-ring; tail is more reddish brown than the rest of the bird.

HABITAT
Is found in a wide variety of woodland types, including coniferous, deciduous and mixed forests, low wooded swamps and recently cut and burned-over areas.

The range of the hermit thrush

BEHAVIOR
Forages on the ground, gleaning insects from among dead leaves and low foliage. Will also hover and pick insects from twigs or leaves. Can be quite tame and easy to approach. Frequently "flicks" its wings while perched, and will raise and lower its tail when disturbed. Flight is direct and fast like a robin's.

CALLS
The song is a haunting series of clear flute or bell-like tones rising through delicate ringing notes and fading at the end to a silvery tinkling. The call is a short *chuk*.

FOOD
Diet includes insects, insect larvae and eggs, spiders, earthworms, snails and other invertebrates. Berries and some fruit are also taken, particularly during fall migration.

This hermit thrush is in its typical habitat, deep within the northern woods.

THRUSHES

FAMILY LIFE
Monogamous pair; the female builds a cup-shaped nest of twigs, leaves, bark, moss, grass, occasionally using some mud, on the ground or in the low branch of a tree. The typical clutch of 4 eggs is incubated by the female for 12 or 13 days. The altricial young remain in the nest for 12 days and are fed by both parents. Two broods per year.

MIGRATION
Spring birds usually arrive on their breeding grounds from early April to mid-May. Fall migration generally occurs between late August and mid-October.

CONSERVATION CONCERNS
Species status overall in North America is *secure* in the United States and Canada. Forest fragmentation poses a threat. However, because it does not winter exclusively in the tropics like other North American forest thrushes, it may not be as severely affected by neotropical deforestation as closely related species.

A conservation status map of the hermit thrush

RELATED SPECIES
One of 5 brown forest thrushes in North America, all of which belong to the genus *Catharus*. All are known for their beautiful songs.

VEERY

(Catharus fuscescens)

The reddish back distinguishes the veery from other thrushes

This seldom-seen thrush is best known by the cascading ethereal song that is performed by the male at dusk.

APPEARANCE
Length: 7.5 inches. *Wingspan:* 11.5 inches. Reddish brown upperparts; underparts are whitish gray with gray flanks; dark upper mandible, lighter lower mandible; faint reddish brown spots on breast; long, slender, pinkish legs.

HABITAT

Inhabits moist, relatively young second growth woodlands, especially willow, alder and poplar with a dense understory. Is often near wet areas such as streams or swamps.

The range of the veery

BEHAVIOR

Forages mostly on the ground, gleaning food by flipping over leaf litter with its bill. Also feeds in trees and foliage and hawks for flying insects. Often perches on a low branch, log or rock near the water searching for prey that it will swoop at to capture. Is generally shy and secretive. Moves on the ground using long hops. Flight is direct with steadily beating wings.

CALLS

Song is a rich, flute-like (almost harmonic sounding) down-slurred series of rolling notes *whee-you, whee-you, whee-you, re-ah, re-ah.* Call is a descending *whee-you.*

Because they spend so much time deep in the tangled understory of dense young woods, the veery is rarely seen

FOOD
Diet consists of insects, insect larvae, spiders and other inverte-brates, and, especially in fall and winter, fruits and berries.

FAMILY LIFE
Monogamous pair; the female builds a substantial cup-shaped nest of grass, weed stems, twigs, shredded bark and moss lined with dry leaves and soft bark. The nest is placed on a mound of vegetation on the ground beneath a shrub or a bush, or occasion-ally off the ground in a low shrub. The typical clutch of 3 to 5 eggs is incubated by the female for 10 to 12 days. Altricial young remain in the nest for 10 days and are fed by both parents. One or 2 broods per year.

MIGRATION
Usually arrives on its breeding grounds from late April to early May. Fall migration generally occurs from mid-August to late September.

CONSERVATION CONCERNS
Species status overall in North America is *secure* in the United States and Canada. It has declined in eastern North America over the last 30 years or more, but is still widespread and common. Fragmentation of forests and increased browsing of the understory by white-tailed deer may be threats. The impact on the population caused by rapid deforestation of wintering grounds in southern Brazil is still unknown.

RELATED SPECIES
In North America, it is one of five brown spotted thrushes, includ-ing the hermit, Swainson's, gray-cheeked and Bicknell's, all of which are known for their beautiful songs and belong to the genus *Catharus*.

THRUSHES

BICKNELL'S THRUSH

(Catharus bicknelli)

A Bicknell's thrush sings its distinctive thin, flute-like song

Long considered a subspecies of the more widespread gray-cheeked thrush, the quite rare Bicknell's thrush was only recognized as a separate species in 1995.

APPEARANCE
Length: 6.75 inches. *Wingspan:* 11.5 inches. Overall olive-brown above with a gray-brown face; partial eye-ring is often indistinct; tip of bill is black with lower mandible showing yellow; spotted breast and a whitish belly; edge feathers of tail are a warm rufous color; long legs; safely distinguishable from the very similar gray-cheeked only by song and range.

HABITAT

Is found in patchily distributed high elevation montane and maritime forests that are dominated by balsam fir with some black and red spruce, as well as white birch and mountain ash. Prefers areas with old dead trees surrounded by younger forest. Often inhabits disturbed areas that are regenerating after severe wind, ice or fire damage. Generally breeds above 3,000 feet in the southern part of its range in the Catskill

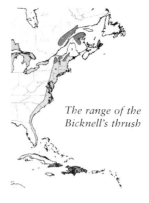

The range of the Bicknell's thrush

Mountains and at progressively lower elevations to the north.

BEHAVIOR

A very secretive bird that is active largely at dawn and dusk, the Bicknell's thrush is one of the least known of all North American woodland bird species. Very versatile in its foraging habits, it is generally found feeding either low in the trees or on the ground. Gleans insects from foliage and branches. Like a robin, it will search for insects on the ground by hopping and stopping and peering carefully. It also uses its feet to scratch in the leaf litter in search of prey. Is known to hawk flying insects from a perch. Moves with agility on the ground by hopping. Flight is fairly rapid and direct with steady wing beats.

CALLS

The song is a descending series of spiralling, thin, flute-like phrases similar to the veery, but higher, thinner and more nasal in tone. Call is a high, thin *kyeer*.

FOOD

Diet includes insects (predominantly beetles), caterpillars, other insect larvae and eggs and some invertebrates such as spiders and snails. Also takes some berries and fruits, particularly in the fall.

FAMILY LIFE

Monogamous pair; the female builds a bulky cup-shaped nest of twigs, leaves, bark strips, grass and moss, with or without a scant lining of leaves and other fine plant material, which is usually placed near the trunk on a low horizontal tree branch in scrubby stands of fir, often near a forest edge. The typical clutch of 3 or 4 eggs is incubated by the female for 9 to 14 days. Altricial young remain in the nest for 9 to 13 days and are fed by both parents. One brood (rarely 2) per year.

MIGRATION

Though there is little data for breeders in the northern part of the range, it appears that birds usually arrive on their breeding grounds between late May and mid-June. Fall migration generally occurs between mid-September and late October.

CONSERVATION CONCERNS

Species status overall for North America is only *apparently secure* in the United States and *vulnerable* in Canada. With a total population of only about 50,000 birds, it is one of the rarest woodland species in

A conservation status map of the Bicknell's thrush

North America. Both its breeding range and wintering range are limited (it winters only on 4 islands in the Greater Antilles in the Caribbean), putting the species at risk of extinction in the future.

RELATED SPECIES

One of 5 North American thrushes that are members of the *Catharus* genus, it was once considered a subspecies of the gray-cheeked thrush.

GRAY CATBIRD
(Dumetella carolinensis)

A gray catbird scolds from the safety of a thicket

Chances are that if you hear strange mewing noises emanating from low in the dense bushes or undergrowth, a catbird is gently scolding you.

APPEARANCE
Length: 8.5 inches. *Wingspan:* 11 inches. A slim bird that is over-all slate gray with upperparts that are darker than its underparts; head has a black cap and the bill is short and dark; the eye is black; the long black tail has reddish brown undertail feathers and is often flicked from side to side.

HABITAT

Dumetella, the bird's genus name, means "small thicket." Prefers brushy thickets with tangled vegetation that are often located next to swamp marshes or other wet areas. Is also found in forest edges, suburban parks and dense hedges, often close to human habitation. Is absent from areas deep within the forest.

The range of the gray catbird

BEHAVIOR

Forages by gleaning food from the ground or from foliage and branches. Is usually difficult to see as it spends much of its time on or near the ground in the middle of bushes. Is very tame and will respond readily to a *pish-pish-pish* birder's call, often approaching extremely closely. Will mount a very strong defense of its nesting area. Generally sings from an exposed perch. Is one of the few North American birds that occasionally sings at night. Flight is direct and swift on rapidly beating wings.

A gray catbird

CALLS

Because its vocal organ is able to operate two sides independently of one another, the catbird is able to produce songs of great complexity. The song is an irregular rambling series of whistles, chirps, mews, whines and squeaks strung together in a long-winded chorus. Will often imitate the songs of other birds. The call is a simple *mew* as well as an abrupt *chit*.

FOOD
Diet includes insects, caterpillars, spiders and other invertebrates, as well as a fair percentage of berries and fruit, which accounts for up to 50 percent of its intake at times.

FAMILY LIFE
Monogamous pair; both sexes (mostly the female) build a cup-shaped nest of grasses, twigs, plant fibers and leaves, lined with fine material and placed in a shrub or tree, usually quite close to the ground. The typical clutch of 4 eggs is incubated by the female for 12 to 13 days. Altricial young remain in the nest for 10 or 11 days and are fed mostly by the male. Two broods per year.

MIGRATION
It is a late spring migrant. Birds arrive on their breeding grounds from early May to early June. Fall migration generally occurs between late August and September. Some coastal birds are year-round residents.

CONSERVATION CONCERNS
Species status overall in North America is *secure* in the United States and Canada with a declining population in the southeastern United States.

RELATED SPECIES
One of 10 members of the family *Mimidae* (made up of the catbird, thrashers and the northern mockingbird) that regularly occur in North America. It is the only member of its genus *Dumetella*.

MIMIDS

NORTHERN MOCKINGBIRD

(*Mimus polyglottos*)

The long tail is apparent on this northern mockingbird

This scientific name of this indefatigable songster, *polyglottos* ("many-tongued"), couldn't be more appropriate as it spills forth a veritable symphony of other birds' music.

APPEARANCE
Length: 10 inches. *Wingspan:* 14 inches. Is a robin-sized bird; overall medium gray upperparts, thin dark eye-line, wings with distinctive wingbars; whitish underparts; long black legs. In flight its brilliant white wing patches are visible.

HABITAT

Is a real generalist that is found in a wide variety of habitats, the only requirement being that they are open or semi-open areas with some trees, bushes and dense shrubbery. Appears to be more common in areas of human habitation than they are in the wild, where they are found at the edges of woodlands and clearings and in second growth.

The range of the northern mockingbird

BEHAVIOR

Usually forages on the ground where it will lift its wings up in a quick jerking motion to flash its white wing patches, thus frightening insects into the open. Commonly hunts insects on freshly mown grass. Gleans prey from twigs and foliage and will take berries and other fruit. Vigorously defends nesting territory and will often attack larger birds and mammals. Unmated males are one of the few North American birds that sing at night. Short flights are undulating with flapping and gliding, and longer flights are steady on strongly beating wings.

CALLS

A male's repertoire can contain up to 150 song types of other species, as well as other mimicked sounds such as machinery, mechanical noises and the vocalizations of non-bird species. Some of its phrases are original and not mimicked. Each phrase in a mockingbird's song series is repeated 2 to 6 or more times. As an individual grows, the repertoire can change and grow in size. Will also whisper a barely audible song at times. The call is a harsh *chack*.

FOOD

Diet includes a wide variety of insects, spiders and other invertebrates such as crayfish. Also takes a considerable amount of fruits and berries. Small vertebrates may be taken on rare occasions.

A *northern mockingbird*

FAMILY LIFE

Pair is generally monogamous, although occasionally males or females may breed with more than one mate. Both sexes build a cup-shaped nest of twigs, stems and shredded bark that is usually placed in the fork of a shrub or tree usually not far from the ground. Typical clutch of 3 to 5 eggs is incubated by the female for 12 or 13 days. Altricial young remain in the nest for 11 to 13 days and are fed by both parents. Two or 3 broods per year.

MIGRATION

Is generally a year-round resident, although it is believed that some northern birds may migrate.

CONSERVATION CONCERNS

Species status overall in North America is *secure* in the United States and only *apparently secure* in Canada where numbers are traditionally low due to a limited range. May be in decline throughout the continent.

RELATED SPECIES

Is 1 of 10 species belonging to the family *Mimidae* that regularly occurs in North America, and the only member of the genus *Mimus*.

BROWN
THRASHER

(Toxostoma rufum)

A brown thrasher snacks on a grapefruit at a feeder

This large, ground-loving bird is the most widespread species of thrasher, inhabiting most of the southern half of the continent.

APPEARANCE
Length: 11.5 inches. *Wingspan:* 13 inches. Reddish brown (the color of a red fox) above, white below with bold dark streaking; very long tail and long legs; bill is fairly long and curved downward slightly; yellow eyes; faint white wingbars.

HABITAT
Brushy areas, the edges of deciduous forests, hedgerows, dry thickets and wooded or shrubby suburbs.

BEHAVIOR

Long legs are well adapted to walking and running on the ground. Forages mostly on the ground where it uses a quick side-to-side motion of its long, curved bill to sweep leaf litter aside to capture insects. Also probes or digs in the soil for prey. Will glean insects from foliage low in trees or bushes. Flight is rapid with quick, shallow wing beats. Short flights are somewhat undulating with alternating flapping and gliding.

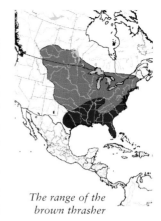

The range of the brown thrasher

CALLS

The male brown thrasher has one of the largest repertoires of any North American songbird with over 1,000 songs. The typical song is a musical series of double notes, rich and varied, and almost conversational in effect. Of the brown thrasher's song Henry David Thoreau wrote: "He says *cherruwit, cherruwit, go ahead, go ahead, give it to him;* etc., etc., etc." Couldn't have said it better myself. The call is a loud *chack.*

FOOD

Diet includes insects and other invertebrates, frogs, salamanders, seeds, berries, fruits and nuts.

FAMILY LIFE

Monogamous pair; the male and female build a cup-shaped nest of twigs, dead leaves and grass, usually in low bushes, vines and shrubs and occasionally on the ground. The typical clutch of 3 to 5 eggs is incubated by both sexes for 11 to 14 days. Altricial young remain in the nest for 9 to 13 days and are fed by both parents. Two or 3 broods per year.

A brown thrasher showing its spotted breast

MIGRATION
Spring migrants usually arrive on breeding grounds in early April to early May. Fall migration generally occurs in late August to early October.

CONSERVATION CONCERNS
Species status overall in North America is *secure* in the United States and Canada.

RELATED SPECIES
One of 8 species of thrashers in North America, and the only one found in the eastern half of the continent. All belong to the genus *Toxostoma.*

CEDAR WAXWING
(*Bombycilla cedrorum*)

Cedar waxwings are striking birds

These exotic-looking, nomadic birds mysteriously show up by the hundreds in search of berries during migration, only to quickly move on to a new area once they've eaten them all.

APPEARANCE
Length: 7 inches. *Wingspan:* 12 inches. Overall light brown (has a very smooth appearance as if it were dipped in milk chocolate) with an unmistakable crest and black mask; belly is a pale brownish-yellow and tip of tail is a vibrant yellow. The brilliant small waxy red tips on the secondary flight feathers of mature adult birds are not always apparent. The only other bird that this species could be confused with is the bohemian waxwing, which is larger and has a darker gray belly and rufous undertail feathers.

HABITAT

Lives in deciduous, coniferous and mixed woodlands, forest edges and treed parks. Is often seen in fruit-bearing trees near human habitation.

BEHAVIOR

Is gregarious, usually found in flocks and quite tame. Large flocks will often forage on berries by climbing about the branches and plucking. Are tolerant of feeding very close to each other. Will

The range of the cedar waxwing

often pick berries off ground. Berries are often passed from bird to bird. It is not uncommon to see gluttonous birds become so over-stuffed on berries that they are unable to fly. It hawks for insects such as mayflies in the spring. Flight is strong and slightly undulating with rapid wing beats alternating with brief gliding with wings pulled against the body.

CALLS

The call is a very thin, high-pitched *zreeee*.

FOOD

Diet consists mostly of berries, but also eats flowers and tree sap. In the spring insects are taken primarily to be fed to young.

FAMILY LIFE

Monogamous pair; will occasionally nest in loose colonies. The male and the female build the nest, which can be either relatively flat or cup-shaped. The typical clutch of 3 to 5 eggs is incubated by both sexes for 12 to 16 days. Altricial young remain in the nest for 14 to 18 days and are fed by both parents. One or 2 broods per year.

A cedar waxwing checks out some withered berries

MIGRATION

Some believe that the spring migration of the cedar waxwing occurs in 2 separate surges, one in February and March, and a later one in May to early June. The evidence for this is not conclusive, however, and most agree on the latter dates for spring migration. In the fall, migration generally occurs from late August to October.

CONSERVATION CONCERNS

Species status overall in North America is *secure* in the United States and Canada with the population possibly on the rise. The reason for its growing numbers is likely to due widespread forestry that results in the "patchy" successional habitats that are ideal for berry-producing shrubs and trees.

RELATED SPECIES

The only other species in North America belonging to the genus *Bombycilla* is the bohemian waxwing.

BLUE JAY
(Cyanocitta cristata)

A blue jay in flight showing the intricate structure of its wing feathers

This small member of the Corvid family is one of the boldest, most conspicuous of all North American birds. The blue jay is a pleasure to behold with its brilliant plumage and raucous personality.

APPEARANCE
Length: 11 inches. *Wingspan:* 16 inches. Is an unmistakable, large songbird with a bright blue back, crown and wings with bold white wingbars and patches; tail is long with black barring and white feathers on outer tips; white face and belly with light gray breast and sides; distinctive black necklace; long, black, chisel-shaped bill.

HABITAT

Mixed coniferous and deciduous forest, deciduous woodlands, open forest, city parks, residential areas with shade trees and fragmented forest areas. The species was once largely found in natural forests, but has adapted well to a variety of human-altered landscapes.

The range of
the blue jay

BEHAVIOR

Is usually found in small, boisterous flocks after the breeding season and in winter. Very much a generalist, the blue jay forages on the ground for both plant and animal food. Will hawk for flying insects. Is notorious as an inveterate nest robber, taking both the eggs and young birds of other species. Buries many more acorns than it can eat, and is thus an important ecological factor in the health and regeneration of beech and oak forests. Will occasionally aggressively appropriate the nests of other songbird species. Flight is fast and direct, with steady rowing-like wing beats.

CALLS

The song is a loud, grating *jay-jay-jay* or a softer *tweedle-tweedle*. Imitates several species of forest hawks, including the red-shouldered hawk. Audubon wrote of the blue jay's "mischievous disposition" when referring to its penchant for imitating the cries of sharp-shinned hawks to scare away smaller songbirds.

FOOD

Eats just about anything it can handle. Majority of diet consists of plant food, including acorns, nuts, seeds and fruit. Will eat a variety of invertebrates such as insects, spiders and caterpillars and vertebrates including small rodents, nestling birds, bird eggs, fish, frogs and reptiles.

A blue jay in autumn foliage

FAMILY LIFE

Monogamous pair; both sexes build a cup-shaped nest of sticks, bark, twigs, moss, lichens and human-made items such as string, paper and cloth. Lined with soft material, the nest is usually placed in trees or shrubs on a branch near the trunk or in the crotch of a tree, and occasionally built in a tangle of vines. The typical clutch of 4 or 5 eggs is incubated by both sexes (mostly the female) for 16 to 18 days. The altricial young remain in the nest for 17 to 21 days and are fed by both parents. One to 3 broods per year.

MIGRATION

Year-round resident throughout much of its range. Migrants usually arrive on their breeding grounds between late April to late May. Fall migration generally occurs between mid-September and late October.

CONSERVATION CONCERNS

Species status overall in North America is *secure* in the United States and Canada. Population may be declining.

RELATED SPECIES

One of 11 jay species (including the Clark's nutcracker) in North America and 1 of 2 members of the genus *Cynaocitta*, the other being the Stellar's jay.

Did You Know?

The shape of a bird's wing can be a clue to how it lives. Many woodland birds such as songbirds, woodpeckers, grouse and doves have wings that are relatively wide compared to their length  (known as a low aspect ratio). This characteristic gives these birds the ability to take off quickly and maneuver efficiently, twisting this way and that to avoid crashing into branches and trees. Birds of prey that hunt in the confines of the forest also have such wings to enable them to rapidly negotiate between the trees while pursuing their quarry. Other species such as falcons, nighthawks and swallows have slender, pointed wings that are relatively narrower compared to length. These are specialists in rapid, sustained flight in open areas.

GREEN JAY
(*Cyanocorax yncas*)

The green jay is the only large brilliant green North American bird

This beautiful tropical jay reaches the northernmost part of its North American range in southern Texas where it is common, conspicuous and unmistakable.

APPEARANCE
Length: 10.5 inches. *Wingspan:* 13.5 inches. Green back and wings; tail green with yellow outer feathers; head, cheeks and eyebrows are purplish-blue with a white forehead patch; heavy black "beard" runs down the side of the head and covers chin and upper breast; underparts are olive-green and yellow.

HABITAT

A variety of forest and scrub habitats, including riparian and pine-oak woodlands and thickets, treed residential areas and parks.

The range of the green jay

BEHAVIOR

Forages in family groups among branches and foliage, gleans food from the ground and rarely hawks for flying insects. Will usually begin at the bottom of a tree and work its way, spiralling around and up the tree, to the top. Frequently hangs upside down when gleaning food from the tips of smaller branches. Occasionally hovers to inspect food locations such as clumps of Spanish moss. Contact calls given every 15 to 30 seconds between family members when foraging. Will use twigs as tools to extract insects from under bark. Flight is undulating with alternating flapping and gliding.

CALLS

Calls are varied, from harsh screams of alarm to the bell-like flight call to the commonly heard *cheek-cheek-cheek-cheek* call.

FOOD

Varied diet includes insects, spiders and other invertebrates, rodents, frogs, lizards, young birds and eggs, seeds, nuts and fruit.

The tropical-colored green jay in its southern habitat

A deep blue-and-black head caps off the spectacular green plumage of the green jay's body

FAMILY LIFE

Monogamous pair with family group of 4 to 9 birds. Both sexes participate in building a cup-shaped nest of thorny twigs, with a soft nest cup of moss, rootlets, grass and leaves placed off the ground in a shrub or small tree in a dense thicket. The typical clutch of 3 to 5 eggs is incubated by the female for 17 to 18 days. Altricial young remain in the nest for 19 days and are fed by both parents. One brood per year.

MIGRATION

Year-round resident.

CONSERVATION CONCERNS

Species status overall in North America is only *apparently secure* in the United States due to its restricted range.

RELATED SPECIES

The only member of the genus *Cyanocorax*.

WESTERN SCRUB-JAY

(Aphelocoma californica)

*A slender body, long tail and lovely coloration
distinguish the western scrub-jay*

This familiar slender bird with its long tail and raucous voice is the western equivalent of the ubiquitous eastern blue jay.

APPEARANCE

Length: 11.5 inches. *Wingspan:* 16 inches. Wings and tail are bright blue; back is gray; blue nape of neck, crown and forehead; thin white eyebrow; dark gray cheek patch; white throat with blue "necklace"; grayish-white underparts. Birds of the interior are lighter overall and less bold than their coastal counterparts.

HABITAT

Inhabits pine-oak woodlands, scrub (oak, juniper and pinyon), riparian thickets, chaparral, residential areas with trees and natural cover and parks.

BEHAVIOR

Forages mostly on the ground, but also among foliage and branches. Is usually seen in small flocks or pairs. Pilfers food from acorn woodpecker granary trees and makes its own cache. Its habit of burying the seeds of oaks and pinyon pines then forgetting to retrieve them makes the scrub-jay an important factor in maintaining and helping to propagate these tree species. Is very tame and bold, frequenting bird feeders. Lands on deer to pick ticks off their backs. Flight is direct and buoyant with steady wing beats.

The range of the western scrub-jay

CALLS

Calls are varied, loud and distinctive. Commonly heard calls are a grating, harsh *sreeep* or a rapid series *wek-wek-wek*.

FOOD

Diet is quite varied and includes mostly insects, spiders and other invertebrates, small mammals, reptiles and amphibians, young birds and birds eggs, nuts, fruits, acorns and seeds.

A western scrub-jay

FAMILY LIFE

Monogamous pair; both sexes participate in building a cup-shaped nest of twigs, grass and moss, lined with soft materials such as rootlets and hair that is placed in a dense shrub or tree at least 2 feet off the ground or higher. The typical clutch of 3 to 6 eggs is incubated by the female for 15 to 17 days. Altricial young remain in the nest for 18 to 19 days and are fed by both parents. One brood per year.

MIGRATION

Year-round resident. Occasionally will wander in search of food.

CONSERVATION CONCERNS

Species status overall for North America is *secure* in the United States. Subspecies *A.c. cana*, found only in the Eagle Mountains in California, is listed as a California State Species of Special Concern because of its limited range.

A conservation status map of the western scrub-jay

RELATED SPECIES

One of 4 North American jays, including the Florida scrub, island scrub and Mexican jays that belong to the genus *Aphelocoma*. The western scrub-jay and Florida scrub-jay were once thought to be a single species.

FLORIDA SCRUB-JAY

(*Aphelocoma coerulescens*)

The Florida scrub-jay is threatened by loss of its habitat

The only bird species whose range is restricted entirely to the Sunshine State, this intelligent, very tame bird is being squeezed out of the last remnants of its habitat by development and an exploding human population.

APPEARANCE
Length: 11.5 inches. *Wingspan:* 13.5 inches. Wings and tail bright blue; back is gray; nape of neck, crown and cheek are blue; white forehead continuous with heavy white eyebrow; white throat with blue "necklace"; pale grayish-brown underparts.

HABITAT

Has a very restricted habitat. Lives exclusively in oak-scrub that grows on the well-drained sandy soils that are thinly scattered throughout Florida. Even large tracts of pine, grass plains and hammocks adjacent to scrub-jay habitat aren't used by the bird. Rarely travels more than a mile or two from where it was born.

The range of the Florida scrub-jay

BEHAVIOR

Forages mostly on the ground, but also among foliage and branches. Pushes into tight spaces under vegetation where it probes emerging or dead palmetto fronds to find prey. Also pecks open acorns. Rakes aside leaf litter with bill to find food. Occasionally deliberately crashes though vegetation to flush insects. Is usually

The threatened Florida scrub-jay in its habitat on Merritt Island, Florida

seen in small family flocks or pairs. Caches acorns to be eaten in late winter or early spring when insects are scarce. Highly intelligent and one of the tamest of North American birds, it will perch on a person's hand, head or shoulder when food is offered. Hops, and occasionally walks or runs on ground. Flight is direct with steady wing beats similar but somewhat weaker than the western scrub-jay.

CALLS
Similar to western scrub-jay with a loud, harsh quality. Most commonly heard is an ascending *creeech* and many other variations.

FOOD
Diet consists of invertebrates such as grasshoppers, crickets, caterpillars and spiders. Also takes vertebrates such as frogs, lizards and small snakes. Acorns (an important food), berries and seeds are also taken.

FAMILY LIFE
Monogamous pair with help from family group; both sexes participate in building a cup-shaped nest with an outer basket of thorny twigs and an inner basket of smaller twigs and fine materials such as rootlets, lined with the fibers of palmettos and rootlets and placed low in a dense shrub or tree, most often a scrub oak. The typical clutch of 3 to 5 eggs is incubated by the female for 17 to 19 days. Altricial young remain in the nest for 18 days and are fed by both parents, which are usually helped in feeding by prebreeding age offspring from the previous year. Studies have shown that a pair with such help throughout their breeding lives produce more offspring overall. One or 2 broods per year.

MIGRATION
Year-round resident. Is one of the most sedentary of North American birds, rarely straying more than a few miles from its area of birth.

CONSERVATION CONCERNS

Species status overall in North America is *imperiled*. Exists only in Florida. Federally listed under the Endangered Species Act as "Threatened." Cause of severe population decline is loss of oak-scrub habitat to agriculture and real estate development. Suppression of natural fires also causes

A conservation status map of the Florida scrub-jay

a deleterious change in the habitat by allowing an increase in pine trees, rendering it unsuitable for scrub-jays. Up to 80 percent of the species' entire population lives on 2 tracts of federal land, Merritt Island National Wildlife Refuge and Ocala National Forest.

RELATED SPECIES

One of 4 North American jays, including the western scrub, island scrub and Mexican jay, that belong to the genus *Aphelocoma*. The Florida scrub-jay and the western scrub-jay were once thought to be a single species.

GRAY JAY
(*Perisoreus canadensis*)

Known as a "camp robber," the gray jay can often be seen perched on trees just above the heads of campers

Because of its personality and appearance, this bold, inquisitive bird is reminiscent of an oversized chickadee.

APPEARANCE
Length: 11.5 inches. *Wingspan:* 18 inches. Slightly larger than a blue jay; gray overall, darker on top with a black cap, white face, large dark eyes and a short bill; feathers appear fluffy; long tail; juvenile is dark gray with small white stripe on its face.

HABITAT
Lives in coniferous and mixed coniferous-deciduous forests, open woodland and bogs of boreal and subalpine regions.

BEHAVIOR

Bold and tame, displaying little or no fear of humans. The gray jay is best known as a "camp robber" for its habit of stealing anything from food items to shiny utensils. In the wild, it forages both on the ground and among the foliage of trees. Produces large amounts of a sticky saliva that is used to "glue" pieces of food to trees as a cache that will be used by the pair throughout the winter and at other times. These caches are often raided by blue jays and Stellar's jays. Flight is buoyant with steadily flapping wings.

The range of the gray jay

CALLS

Though not as noisy as most jays, the gray jay has a variety of vocalizations. Most commonly heard is a soft whistled *quee-oo* that drops in pitch. Also utters a variety of low chuckling sounds, a harsh *kah-wee* cry, as well as mimicking other species such as smaller songbirds and raptors.

FOOD

Like the blue jay, the gray jay is a generalist taking a wide variety of food, including acorns, seeds, fruit, berries, insects, invertebrates, small mammals, eggs and young of other bird species, as well as carrion.

A young gray jay in immature plumage

FAMILY LIFE

Monogamous pair; breeds in small colonies. Along with the great horned owl, the gray jay is one of the earliest breeders in North America, nesting in late winter and incubating eggs in temperatures as cold as −22°F. Both sexes build a bulky, well-made cup-shaped nest of sticks, moss, strips of bark and grass that is held together with spider silk and insect cocoons and is insulated against the extreme cold by a lining of feathers, bark and fur. It is placed on a horizontal branch or in a fork of a coniferous tree, occasionally in a deciduous tree. The typical clutch of 3 or 4 eggs is incubated by the female for 16 to 18 days. Altricial young remain in the nest for 15 to 21 days and are fed by both parents. One brood per year. Despite the extremely early nesting date, gray jays do not attempt a second brood during the warmer spring season.

MIGRATION

Permanent year-round resident.

CONSERVATION CONCERNS

Species status overall in North America is *secure* in the United States and Canada. Despite its tameness, it is a bird that relishes wilderness. Due to extensive logging operations in the boreal forest and the forest fragmentation that accompanies it, the gray jay may come under threat in the future.

RELATED SPECIES

One of 11 jay species (including the Clark's nutcracker) in North America, it is the sole species in the genus *Perisoreus*.

COMMON RAVEN

(*Corvus corax*)

*A common raven, the largest of the songbirds, performs
one of its many vocalizations*

The largest of the world's songbirds, the common raven is important in mythology and rich in intelligence, as well as being of the widest ranging species on the planet.

APPEARANCE

Length: 24 inches. *Wingspan:* Up to 56 inches. A very large, all glossy black, hawk-sized bird distinguished from a crow by its wedge-shaped tail, long heavy bill, shaggy throat feathers and primary feathers that are more pronounced in flight. Unlike the shallow "V" position of a crow's wings, the raven holds them very flat in flight.

HABITAT

Favours forested wilderness areas, Arctic taiga and tundra (as far north as land goes in the northern hemisphere, not far from the North Pole), mountainous regions and along coasts. Is also adaptable to a variety of human-altered habitats, the raven exists almost anywhere on the continent it hasn't been deliberately exterminated by man. Is becoming re-established in forests of the eastern United States where it was formerly extirpated.

The range of the common raven

BEHAVIOR

Entire volumes have been written on the behavior of this most intelligent and complex of birds. Actively forages on ground and in trees for a variety of food items. Hunts in the manner of a hawk for much of its animal prey, often cooperatively in groups. Drops shellfish onto rocks from a great height to break them open. Is an important scavenger of large mammal carrion, playing the same role as the turkey vulture; also scavenges at garbage dumps. Often patrols roads and highways for the roadkill that has become an important food source for them in populated areas. Is a quick learner that can adapt to novel situations and challenges, such as opening picnic chests and food packaging. Engages in play, both in the air and on the ground, such as sliding down snowbanks on its back. Associates closely with wolves, often feeding off their leftovers after a kill, but also apparently leading them to prey that will later be scavenged once the wolves are done with it. Within its range it withstands the harshest of conditions from −40°F Arctic cold to scorching 122°F desert heat. Walks quite efficiently. Flight is very strong on steady beating wings alternating with glides. Soars on thermals like a hawk. In play with other ravens, it is capable of spectacular acrobatic displays such as dives and rolls.

A common raven in flight

CALLS

Largest repertoire of vocalizations of any North American bird, from a deep, guttural croak, to a repetitive *tok-tok-tok*, to clear, bell-like tones.

FOOD

Omnivorous, eating just about anything it can get down—carrion, small mammals, birds, birds' eggs (especially at seabird colonies), fish, shellfish, crustaceans, insects and other terrestrial invertebrates, seeds, acorns, fruit and garbage.

FAMILY LIFE

Monogamous pair; may mate for life. Both sexes build a large nest of heavy sticks and twigs with an inner basket of smaller twigs, lined with fur, moss, animal hair, seaweed, grass and bark chips placed high up in a tree (usually a conifer), on a cliff ledge or on a human-made structure. The typical clutch of 4 to 6 eggs is incubated by the female for 18 to 21 days. Male feeds incubating female. The altricial young remain in the nest for 38 to 44 days and are fed by both parents. May attempt a smaller second brood if the first one fails.

MIGRATION
Year-round resident.

CONSERVATION CONCERNS
Species status overall in North America is *secure* in the United States and Canada. Extirpated from Alabama and endangered in Tennessee. Logging caused declines in many areas, including the disappearance from Pennsylvania and Virginia in the early twentieth century. Is still uncommon, but increasing in former ranges throughout the continent.

RELATED SPECIES
Is 1 of 5 breeding species that belong to the genus *Corvus* in North America.

BLACK-CAPPED CHICKADEE

(Poecile atricapilla)

A black-capped chickadee in a spruce tree

One of the most familiar and widespread of all woodland birds, the charming black-capped chickadee lifts the spirits for thousands of people across the continent who watch its antics at their backyard feeders through the long, northern winters.

APPEARANCE
Length: 5.25 inches. *Wingspan:* 8 inches. Large head; distinctive back cap and chin with a white nape and cheek; gray back and wings with white edges on secondary feathers; long tail; underparts are white with buff-colored sides, flanks and belly.

HABITAT

Inhabits coniferous, deciduous and mixed forests, as well as riparian woodlands, parks, treed residential areas, thickets and orchards.

BEHAVIOR

Is very tame and curious, and it is not uncommon for it to land on a person's hand to be fed. Actively forages on branches, twigs and foliage and will probe under bark. Will often hang

The range of the black-capped chickadee

upside down as it extracts seeds or insects from difficult places. Also hovers and picks insects off surfaces and hawks for flying prey. Uses visual clues such as damaged leaves when looking for caterpillars. Seldom eats food where it is found. Caches each food item individually in its own spot, resulting in a large number of locations to remember. Can remember where food is hidden for 28 days or more. Studies have shown that a part of the brain known as the hippocampus is larger in birds that regularly cache food. In nonbreeding season, it forms small flocks with a social hierarchy.

Will often associate in mixed flocks of kinglets, juncos and red-breasted nuthatches in the winter. Short flights are slow and direct with fluttering wings; longer flights are undulating with alternating fluttering and gliding with wings held to the side.

CALLS

Song is a simple, cheerful phrase *fee-bee-ee* or, put another way, *cheese-bur-ger*, with a brief space between the second and third notes. Also makes many chittering and light gurgling call notes, especially while it is busy feeding, but most commonly heard is the *chicka-dee-dee-dee* call of its name.

A black-capped chickadee comes in to land

FOOD
Diet consist mostly of insects, caterpillars and other invertebrates such as spiders. During the winter it will eat mostly seeds. Sunflower seeds are a favorite at bird feeders.

FAMILY LIFE
Monogamous pair; both sexes participate in excavating or enlarging a tree cavity and lining it with moss, hair, feathers, cocoon silk, plant down and fine vegetation. The nest is placed in a living or dead tree or artificial nesting box at least several feet above the ground. The typical clutch of 6 to 8 eggs is incubated by both sexes for 11 to 13 days. Altricial young remain in the nest for 14 to 18 days and are fed by both parents. One brood per year.

A black-capped chickadee with wings spread for a landing

MIGRATION
Year-round resident. Because they spend winters in extremely harsh and cold conditions, chickadees lower their body temperature at night and go into a regulated hypothermia to conserve energy. Irregular migratory movements of young birds under 1 year old occur every couple of years or so in response to a lack of food.

CONSERVATION CONCERNS
Species status overall for North America is *secure* in the United States and Canada. Species is still abundant and widespread.

RELATED SPECIES
Is 1 of 11 species in North America that belong to the family *Paridae*, the chickadees and titmice. The 7 species of chickadees belong to the genus *Poecile*; the most closely related to the black-capped appears to be the mountain chickadee.

BOREAL CHICKADEE

(Poecile hudsonica)

The boreal chickadee's head is a grayish brown color. It was formerly known as the brown-capped chickadee.

Because of its generally more remote habitat, this delicate looking chickadee is less commonly observed than its bold cousin, the black-capped chickadee.

APPEARANCE

Length: 5.5 inches. *Wingspan:* 8.25 inches. Patterns of markings similar to the black-capped chickadee, but coloration is different and duller. Overall darker gray and brown; wings plain gray; cap is brown, though may appear dark gray or black at a distance; small white cheek patch, gray nape of neck, medium to dark brown sides; long tail; short black bill.

HABITAT

Is primarily an inhabitant of the northern boreal coniferous woods. Occurs north to the treeline. Is also found in northern deciduous and mixed forests.

BEHAVIOR

Like the black-capped variety, it can be bold and curious, and often lives in close proximity to humans. Forages on mid- to high levels in the forest on branches, twigs and foliage. Tends to move to

The range of the boreal chickadee

lower levels as the breeding season progresses. During the winter it will pry into crevices in the bark and search along branches and twigs for hibernating insects. Also hovers and picks insects off surfaces and hawks for flying prey. Is usually found in pairs during the breeding season and in small flocks of 4 to 20 birds at other times of year, and is often found in mixed flocks of kinglets, juncos, other chickadee species and red-breasted nuthatches in the winter. Moves through foliage by hopping from twig to twig and also hops on the ground. Short flights are slow and direct with little undulation; longer flights are somewhat more undulating with alternating fluttering and gliding with wings held to the side.

CALLS

Song is a plain warble or trill with an abrupt first note. Its "chickadee" call is similar, though weaker and more slurred than the black-capped's call and often has a noticeable downward slur at the end, *shee-jay* or *shee-shee-jay-jay*. Also frequently utters *chit* calls and gargling vocalizations.

FOOD

Diet consists mostly of insects, insects' eggs and larvae and other arthropods such as spiders. Also eats seeds and some berries, especially in the winter. Will frequent bird feeders in winter if they are available.

FAMILY LIFE

Monogamous pair; both sexes participate (most work done by the female) in excavating or enlarging a tree cavity and lining it with moss, fur, lichen, inner bark, hair, feathers and fine vegetation placed in a living or dead coniferous tree from 1–30 feet above the ground. The typical clutch of 5 to 8 eggs is incubated by the female for 11 to 16 days. Altricial young remain in the nest for 18 days and are fed by both parents. One brood per year.

The boreal chickadee is similar in habits and appearance to the more common black-capped chickadee

MIGRATION

Is generally a year-round resident; however, short-distance southward movements have been observed in parts of its range. During some years, part of its population may undergo southward irruptions in fall, winter and early spring as the birds search for food sources.

CONSERVATION CONCERNS

Species status overall for North America is *secure* in the United States and Canada. Some concerns have been expressed for the health of its habitat in New Hampshire, Quebec and the Maritime provinces.

RELATED SPECIES

Is 1 of 7 species of chickadees in North America, all belonging to the genus *Poecile*. Recent molecular studies suggest that its closest relative is the gray-headed chickadee (known as the Siberian tit in its Old World range) and the chestnut-backed chickadee.

TUFTED TITMOUSE

(Baeolophus bicolor)

A tufted titmouse

This energetic, chickadee-like songbird, a common resident of mature deciduous forests throughout much of eastern North America, has been expanding its range northward over the past several decades. The black-crested titmouse, now a separate species, was until recently considered a race of the Tufted species.

APPEARANCE

Length: 6.5 inches. *Wingspan:* 10 inches. Tail, back, wings and conspicuous crest are medium gray; face is white with a black forehead and straight black bill; underparts grayish-white with dull rust-colored flanks. The black-crested species is similar with a black crest and a white forehead.

HABITAT

Lives in deciduous and mixed deciduous-coniferous woodlands, scrub, shaded residential areas, parks. The black-crested species lives in riparian woodlands in Texas and southern Oklahoma.

The range of the tufted titmouse

BEHAVIOR

Is an active little bird that forages along branches and foliage as well as gleaning insects from bark, and is often seen hanging upside down as it removes seeds and fruits from trees. Will hold an acorn or a nut against a branch with its feet and hammer at it with its bill to crack it open. Moves about in family groups and forms mixed species flocks during the winter. Is tame and a frequent visitor to bird feeders during the fall and winter. Will cache nuts and seeds, often digging holes in the ground to put them in. Flight is undulating with alternating flapping and holding wings at sides.

CALLS

Song is a series of high whistled 2-note phrases made up of a high and then a lower note *peter-peter-peter-peter*. Has various calls, including a chickadee-like but more wheezing *dee-dee-dee*.

FOOD

Diet includes insects and insect larvae, other invertebrates such as spiders and snails, acorns, nuts and seeds.

FAMILY LIFE

Monogamous pair; mates for life. Male and female participate in building nest in a natural or woodpecker-excavated cavity and also in nesting box. They fill the space of the cavity with leaves, shreds of bark, moss, lichen and grass, and the nest cup is made of soft materials such as animal hair, bits of cloth, string and snakeskin. The typical clutch of 5 to 7 eggs is incubated by the female for 13 or 14 days. Altricial young remain in the nest for 15 to 18 days and are fed by both parents. One or 2 broods per year.

MIGRATION
Year-round resident.

CONSERVATION CONCERNS
Conservation status overall for North America is *secure* in the United States. Is considered *vulnerable* in Canada due to its limited range. Range expanded northward over the past 5 decades. Availability of nesting sites appears to be a factor in limiting the population.

RELATED SPECIES
One of 5 species of titmouse in North America, including the very similar black-crested species (once thought to be the same species), along with the oak, juniper and bridled titmouse. All 5 belong to the genus *Baeolophus*.

The black-crested titmouse, now a separate species, was once considered a race of the tufted titmouse

WHITE-BREASTED NUTHATCH

(*Sitta carolinensis*)

Creeping down a tree trunk head-first, a white-breasted nuthatch searches for food

The largest and most widely distributed of the North American nuthatch species, the white-breasted is a fairly common bird of deciduous woods throughout much of the continent.

APPEARANCE
Length: 5.75 inches. *Wingspan:* 11 inches. A short-tailed bird with blue-gray upperparts, a black nape, crown and forehead; white face, throat, breast and belly; long, slightly upturned and pointed bill. Is distinguished from the red-breasted nuthatch by its lack of an eye-stripe and its white belly.

HABITAT

Lives in deciduous woodlands, but also in mixed deciduous-conifer forest and forest edges. Prefers large mature stands with decaying trees. The availability of cavities for nesting is critical.

The range of the white-breasted nuthatch

BEHAVIOR

The white-breasted nuthatch's (as well as the red-breasted's) habit of creeping headfirst down the trunks of large trees is distinctive. It forages in this manner by probing beneath the bark of the trunk and large branches for food. In an example of tool use, the nuthatch will wedge food items in the crevices of bark to hold them like a vice before chiselling them open with its sharp bill. Roosts at night in large bark crevices in summer and in tree holes in winter. Flight is somewhat weak with rapid wing beats alternating with short periods of gliding with wings held against the body.

CALLS

The song is a seldom heard *whe-whe-whe-whe-whe* series of about a dozen soft notes on the same pitch. The call, a nasal *yank-yank-yank* is more commonly heard.

Quite tame, the white-breasted nuthatch is an easy bird to observe as it goes about its daily business

FOOD
Diet includes insects, insect larvae, pupae and eggs, as well as spiders, acorns, nuts and seeds.

FAMILY LIFE
Monogamous pair; the male and female prepares a natural tree cavity, knot hole, deserted woodpecker's hole or nesting box by lining it with hair, feathers, shredded bark, grass and leaves. The nest can be located from just above the ground to 60 feet in height. The typical clutch of 5 to 8 eggs is incubated for 12 days by the female. Altricial young remain in the nest for 12 days and are fed by both adults. One brood per year.

MIGRATION
Generally a year-round resident.

CONSERVATION CONCERNS
Species status overall in North America is *secure* in the United States and Canada.

RELATED SPECIES
Is 1 of 4 nuthatch species in North America, all belonging to the genus *Sitta*, which also includes the red-breasted, the brownheaded and the pygmy nuthatch.

NUTHATCHES

RED-BREASTED NUTHATCH

(Sitta canadensis)

*A red-breasted nuthatch in a typical
head-down foraging position*

The unique *yank-yank-yank* of the red-breasted nuthatch's "tin horn" call is commonly heard throughout the coniferous forests of the continent.

APPEARANCE
Length: 4.5 inches. *Wingspan:* 8.5 inches. Shape similar to the white-breasted nuthatch, but is much smaller. Upperparts are overall gray, with dark eye-line and white eyebrow; blackish crown, white head and throat; breast and belly are distinctly rust colored; thin, slightly upturned bill.

HABITAT

Unlike other North American nuthatch species, this one shows a strong preference for coniferous forests, but is also found in mixed woodlands, as well as deciduous stands of mature trees. The presence of large, decaying trees is preferred.

BEHAVIOR

This active bird forages by creeping down tree trunks headfirst or upside down along the underside of large branches as it gleans insects from cracks

The range of the red-breasted nuthatch

and crevices in the bark. Quite tame and easy to approach, it can often be fed directly from the hand. In the fall and winter it will often move incessantly through the woods with kinglets and chickadees in search of food. Will wedge hard seeds into a crevice in the bark and hammer them open with its bill. Will cache seeds in winter for future retrieval. Flight is on fluttering wings with alternating short periods of gliding with wings held against the body.

CALLS

Call is a high, nasal *yank-yank-yank*. Like its cousin, the white-breasted nuthatch, its song is a rarely heard series of rapidly repeated notes of the same pitch.

FOOD

Insects, insect larvae and eggs, caterpillars and conifer seeds, along with nuts and seeds of deciduous trees.

FAMILY LIFE

Monogamous pair; male and female (mostly female) excavate a cavity nest, often in the dead stump of a conifer, which is usually placed from 5–40 feet up and lined with soft material such as shredded bark or grass. Will occasionally use deserted woodpecker nests, knothole or a bird box. Sticky balsam or evergreen sap is

NUTHATCHES

sometimes smeared around the opening of the nest by the birds. The purpose of this sticky shield is not known for sure, but it is thought that it deters competitors or predators from entering the nest. The typical clutch of 5 or 6 eggs is incubated by the female for 12 days. Altricial young remain in the nest for 14 to 21 days and are fed by both parents. One brood per year.

MIGRATION
Some populations are nonmigratory residents, who will move to find food when it's scarce. Migratory populations arrive on breeding grounds between March and May. Fall migration usually occurs from early August to October.

CONSERVATION CONCERNS
Species status overall in North America is *secure* in the United States and Canada. Because of its preference for mature stands of trees, it is vulnerable to industrial logging.

RELATED SPECIES
Is 1 of 4 nuthatch species in North America, all of which belong to the genus *Sitta*.

BROWN CREEPER

(*Certhia americana*)

*A brown creeper works its way up a
tree trunk in search of food*

The inconspicuous little bird, the only creeper in North America, is quite uncommon throughout its range. Once one is found, great enjoyment can be had observing its peculiar habits.

APPEARANCE

Length: 5.25 inches. *Wingspan:* 7.75 inches. The creeper's back is a cryptic mottled brown that gives it the look of a piece of the tree bark it spends so much of its time on; white throat and breast with a white line over the eye; bill is slender, long and downward curving; tail is long, stiff and reddish brown.

HABITAT

Lives in mature forest, especially coniferous and coniferous-deciduous woodlands and swampy woodlands. Prefers the presence of dead or dying trees for nesting sites. Groves of mature pine are a favorite foraging habitat for brown creepers.

The range of the brown creeper

BEHAVIOR

The brown creeper's foraging behavior is unique among North American birds. Using its thin, curved bill it gleans insects, their eggs and larvae from the cracks and crevices of the bark. There's no better description of how the bird moves than that of Henry David Thoreau: "It begins at the base, and creeps rapidly upward

by starts, adhering close to the bark and shifting a little from side to side often till near the top, then suddenly darts off downward to the base of another tree, where it repeats the same course." While doing this it uses its long, stiff tail to brace itself against the tree in the manner of a woodpecker. The creeper will also work its way up the trunk in a spiral. Though not often seen, the creeper is quite tame and may allow a fairly close approach. When feeling threatened, it will camouflage itself by flattening itself against the bark, spreading its wings and remaining

A brown creeper shows just how effective its cryptic coloring is as it forages for insects on a tree trunk

still. Flight is strong and direct, and usually short, with rapid wing beats.

CALLS
Song is a high, thin series of notes, *tsee-tsee-situ-tsee*, somewhat similar to the call of a Blackburnian warbler. Call is a thin *tsee*.

FOOD
Diet is made up largely of insects, their eggs and larvae and spiders and other small invertebrates. Also eats some nuts and seeds, and will take suet at feeders.

FAMILY LIFE
Monogamous pair; both sexes build a cup-like nest underneath a large flap of bark or occasionally in a tree hole. Twigs, moss, bark, pine needles, spruce needles and spider silk are used to construct the nest. The typical clutch of 5 or 6 eggs is incubated by the female for 13 to 17 days. The altricial young remain in the nest for 13 to 16 days and are fed by both parents. One brood per year.

MIGRATION
Year-round resident throughout most of its range, with limited migration in places.

CONSERVATION CONCERNS
Species status overall in North America is *secure* in the United States and Canada with significant declines in Oregon and Vermont. Loss of forested wetlands and floodplain woods may be having a negative impact on the population.

RELATED SPECIES
Is the only species of creeper in North America.

BEWICK'S WREN

(*Thryomanes bewickii*)

A Bewick's wren

This once widespread wren, a singer of complex, beautiful songs, has all but disappeared east of the Mississippi and is declining in the West.

APPEARANCE

Length: 5.25 inches. *Wingspan:* 7 inches. Is a small, overall drab little bird with brown upperparts and light gray below (darker in western birds); long thin, slightly downward curving bill and conspicuous white eyebrow; white throat and breast; tail is finely barred and has white corners.

HABITAT

Prefers open woodlands with dense undergrowth, shrublands, upland thickets, river and streamsides, hedgerows and treed suburbs.

The range of the
Bewick's wren

BEHAVIOR

Quite tame and easily approached, this active, noisy wren can be somewhat difficult to pick out because its somewhat cryptic coloration blends so well with its surroundings. It forages by gleaning insects from tree branches, leaves and trunks, seldom more than 10 feet above the ground. Where habitat lacks trees, it will feed on the ground. Holds head high and wags tail incessantly from side to side. Occasionally will attack the nests of other Bewick's wrens as well as other species nesting nearby. Flight is direct on weakly fluttering wings.

CALLS

The song of eastern birds is a complex thin melody of rising buzzes, trills and notes, *see-tew-wee-tee-eee*, somewhat reminiscent of the song sparrow. Males typically have a repertoire of 9 to 22 songs that vary depending on the geographic range. The western song is somewhat simpler than the eastern. The call is a plain *chip*.

FOOD

Eats exclusively insects, insect larvae and eggs, spiders and other small invertebrates; no plant matter.

FAMILY LIFE

Monogamous pair; male and female build a nest in almost any kind of cavity or cavity-like place, including knot holes, hollow logs, rock crevices, the middle of brush piles, mailboxes, abandoned cars and outbuildings. The male will build "dummy" nests within its territory. The typical clutch of 5 to 7 eggs is incubated

A Bewick's wren forages on a tree trunk

by the female for 12 to 16 days. The altricial young remain in the nest for 14 days and are fed by both parents. One or 2 broods per year.

MIGRATION
Year-round resident in the western U.S., British Columbia and central U.S. states. The few birds that survive east of the Mississippi appear to arrive on breeding grounds in late March to late April. Fall migration generally occurs between late September and early November.

CONSERVATION CONCERNS
Species status overall in North America is *secure* in the United States. This *overall* status is deceiving, however. It is declining, especially east of the Mississippi River. Has been nearly extirpated from the Appalachians, and may be gone from the rest of the eastern U.S. soon. Causes are not known, but it is thought that competition with several more aggressive species such as the European starling, the house sparrow, the house wren and the Carolina wren may have contributed to the decline. Pollution

may also be a factor. In Canada, where its range has been historically limited, British Columbia's population appears secure; however, the species has possibly been extirpated in Ontario.

RELATED SPECIES

The Bewick's is 1 of 9 species of wren in North America and the only one belonging to the genus *Thryothorus*.

A conservation status map of the Bewick's wren

Did You Know?

Birds are able to create the beautiful music they do because they have a completely different kind of organ for producing sound than mammals. Our larynx is located at the top of our windpipe and is comprised of muscle-controlled vocal cords that produce sound as air passes over them. Birds, however, possess a syrinx, a bony organ often located in the breast cavity that acts as a resonating chamber for sound produced as air passes over flexible vibrating membranes. The volume of a song can be changed by adjusting the air pressure passing into the syrinx, and the pitch is altered by tensing special muscles that tighten or loosen the membranes. Because the 2 sides of the syrinx can be individually controlled by the muscles, some birds are able to produce 2 "voices" simultaneously, resulting in a rich, musical tone. Is it any wonder we are so taken with the magic of birdsong?

CANYON WREN

(Catherpes mexicanus)

*The plain canyon wren is one of the most musical
of all North American birds*

The clear, loud song of this little-studied species is a joyous sound that echoes through the ravines and valleys of the western part of the continent.

APPEARANCE

Length: 5.75 inches. *Wingspan:* 7.5 inches. Overall chestnut brown with a white throat and breast; the tail is a dark reddish-brown with distinctive black bars and fairly short; the bill is long, thin, and down-curved.

HABITAT

Lives in cliffs, steep-sided canyons and ravines and rocky outcrops, usually in arid areas. Is associated with various vegetation types, including pinyon-juniper, oak woodlands, redwoods, pine, and Douglas fir, and is often found in riparian areas.

The range of the canyon wren

BEHAVIOR

Often sings while foraging among rocks, usually in streams or near water. Uses its flattened head and long, thin bill to thoroughly probe into crevices and pick prey off rock surfaces. Is occasionally observed foraging on human-made stone structures such as barns and bridges. Flight is weak and direct on shallow beating wings.

CALLS

The song is one of the loudest and clearest sung by any North American bird. A tumbling series of silvery, bell-like notes *tsee-tsee-tsee-tsee-tooee-tooee-tooee* descending in pitch and slowing toward the end. Call is a short, metallic buzz.

Typically shy, a canyon wren picks its way along the tangled bank of a southwestern stream

FOOD
Diet includes insects, spiders and other small invertebrates.

FAMILY LIFE
Monogamous pair; the male and female prepare a nest by placing moss, spider webs, leaves, catkins and other soft material on a base of small sticks hidden in a crevice of a rock, under a boulder and occasionally in a building. The typical clutch of 4 to 7 eggs is incubated by the female for 12 to 18 days. Not known how long the altricial young remain in the nest, but they are fed by both parents. Two or 3 broods per year.

MIGRATION
Year-round resident.

CONSERVATION CONCERNS
Species status overall in North America is *secure* in the United States and *vulnerable* in Canada due to its limited range.

RELATED SPECIES
One of 9 species of wrens in North America and the only one in the genus *Catherpes*.

WRENS

VERDIN

(*Auriparus flavipes*)

A verdin in a desert tree

This tiny, active songbird with its loud, persistent call was once abundant in the southwestern United States.

APPEARANCE
Length: 4.5 inches. *Wingspan:* 6.5 inches. Overall pale-gray back and wings and lighter pale-gray underparts; bill is tiny and sharply pointed and the head is yellow; small red patch on the shoulder, often not visible; long tail.

HABITAT
Inhabits primarily desert brushy areas and riparian woods in association with dense thickets of paloverde, acacia, ironwood, mesquite trees and cactus. Is also occasionally found among Joshua trees, tamarisk and oak.

BEHAVIOR

Forages in a similar manner to a chickadee by gleaning insects from foliage and twigs. Also searches for food on tree bark. Uses its feet to hold prey such as caterpillars, then beats them against a hard surface to kill them before eating. Also holds a food item with its feet and tears it with its bill. Will drink nectar from flowers. Seeks shade in midday when temperatures are high. Forages in small, loose flocks during nonbreeding season. Builds a nest for roosting. Is rarely seen on the ground. Flights are generally short on rapidly beating wings.

The range of the verdin

Verdins are very small birds with large heads and tiny bills

CALLS

Song is a somewhat chickadee-like *see-soor-soor.* Most common call is a repetitive, staccato *chip-chip-chip-chip.* Also a single *tseet.*

FOOD

Diet includes insect adults, larvae and eggs, caterpillars, spiders and other tiny invertebrates. Also eats berries and fruits, pulp from seedpods of paloverde, mesquite and ironwood trees and takes nectar from flowers. Frequents hummingbird feeders.

FAMILY LIFE

Monogamous pair; builds 2 types of nests, one for roosting at night and a larger one for breeding. For the breeding nest, both sexes build a conspicuous oval, ball-shaped structure of twigs, grass and leaves held together by spider webs and placed well out toward the end of a branch of a shrub or bush. Very well built, this insulated nest may last several seasons. Typical clutch of 4 eggs is incubated by the female for 14 to 17 days. Altricial young remain in the nest for 18 days and are fed by both adults, mostly the female. Two broods per year.

MIGRATION

Year-round resident.

CONSERVATION CONCERNS

Species status overall in North America is *secure* in the United States. Formerly extremely abundant and still quite common, the verdin's numbers have declined by some 85 percent in the past few decades. Efforts in Texas to protect Bell's vireo's habitat and in California to protect habitat of the black-tailed gnatcatcher may be benefiting the verdin.

RELATED SPECIES

It is the only member of the family *Remizidae* in North America, and is superficially similar to the chickadees, tits and kinglets.

RUBY-CROWNED KINGLET

(Regulus calendula)

This male ruby-crowned kinglet shows the red patch on its head for which it is named

Despite its tiny "birdlet" size, the ruby-crowned kinglet possesses one of the loudest voices heard throughout the northern woods where it makes its home.

APPEARANCE

Length: 4.25 inches. *Wingspan:* 7.25 inches. A very small drab olive-buff bird with a tiny thin bill and a prominent white eye-ring that gives it the appearance that it is staring at you; single bold, white wingbar. The male has a small ruby red crest that is often hard to see.

HABITAT

Is usually found breeding in coniferous (especially boreal areas) or mixed coniferous-deciduous forests. Its breeding habitat ranges well into northern Alaska and Canada's Northwest Territories. During migration and winter it lives in a wide variety of habitats.

The range of the ruby-crowned kinglet

BEHAVIOR

A very active forager that picks insects off branches and foliage, it will often sally forth from a perch and capture insects on the wing, as well as hover and take them off leaves or needles. It constantly flicks wings while foraging. Its small size and quick movements can make it difficult to observe, but it is very tame and will often approach quite closely. Often drinks tree sap that oozes from the feeding holes of sapsuckers. Will join loose feeding flocks of other northern species such as nuthatches, chickadees, golden-crowned kinglets and brown creepers. Flight is undulating with shallow flapping alternated with short glides with wings pulled against the body.

CALLS

The song starts with very thin weak notes, growing in volume into an ebullient outpouring of loud, clear tones *tsee-tsee-tsee, tyew-tyew-tye, hippity-hippity-hippity*. The call is a dry *cheedit*.

FOOD

Eats insects, insect larvae and eggs, small caterpillars, spiders and other tiny invertebrates as well as berries, some seeds and tree sap.

One of the smallest birds of North American woodlands, this ruby-crowned kinglet feeds in a coastal black spruce forest

FAMILY LIFE

Monogamous pair; the female builds a pendulum-shaped nest of moss, lichen, tiny twigs, dead leaves, plant down and spider silk that is lined with fine materials. The nest, which is suspended from a limb from just above the ground to 100 feet up, is open at the top and deep enough to completely hide the incubating bird. The typical clutch of 5 to 11 eggs is incubated by the female for 12 to 14 days. The altricial young remain in the nest for 10 to 16 days and are fed by both parents. One brood per year.

MIGRATION

Spring migrants generally arrive on their breeding grounds during April and May. Fall migration occurs from early September to late October.

CONSERVATION CONCERNS

Species status overall in North America is *secure* in the United States and Canada.

RELATED SPECIES

Belongs to the kinglet family *Regulidae*, of which there is one other species in North America, the golden-crowned kinglet.

BLUE-GRAY GNATCATCHER

(Polioptila caerulea)

A blue-gray gnatcatcher foraging for insects

This widespread, energetic tiny bird is the most common member of the family *Sylviidae* (at one time called the Old World warblers) in North America.

APPEARANCE
Length: 4.5 inches. *Wingspan:* 6 inches. Is very plain; darker slate blue-gray above with light gray underparts; long, conspicuous tail with white outer feathers (appears all white from below) and a bold white eye-ring; male has a thin black line over its eye during breeding season; thin bill.

HABITAT

Inhabits a wide variety of habitats, including deciduous forests, swamplands, open woodlands, brushy growth and riparian woods. Prefers moist areas. In the eastern part of its range it often lives in stands of tall mature trees and in the West it is more often found in scrub and thickets.

The range of the blue-gray gnatcatcher

BEHAVIOR

Extremely energetic and restless, it is constantly flitting high in the trees, usually near the tips of branches. Forages by gleaning insects from twigs and foliage, but also captures them by hovering and occasionally hawking for them by sallying out to snatch insects on the wing. The tail is constantly being fanned and flicked. Flight is weak on fluttering wings.

CALLS

The song is a high, wheezing, warble *zwee-u zwee-u* interspersed by chips and lisps. The call is a high-pitched, rising *swee, swee, swee.*

FOOD

Eats insects, insect larvae and eggs and other small invertebrates such as spiders.

FAMILY LIFE

Monogamous pair; both sexes help build a compact cup-shaped nest of fine plant material such as down and bark, which is held together by spider silk and placed fairly low on a horizontal limb or in the fork of a tree at a height of up to about 25 feet. The typical clutch of 4 to 5 eggs is incubated by the female for 13 days. The altricial young remain in the nest for 10 to 12 days and are fed by both parents. One or 2 broods per year.

MIGRATION

Birds generally arrive on their breeding ground between late April and early May. Fall migration occurs between mid-August and early September. Birds in the extreme southern parts of the range are year-round residents.

CONSERVATION CONCERNS

Species status overall in North America is *secure* in the United States and increasing. In Canada, where its range is limited, it is listed only as *apparently secure* and thought to be declining.

A conservation status map of the blue-gray gnatcatcher

RELATED SPECIES

Four species of gnatcatchers inhabit North America, all of which belong to the genus *Polioptila*, which means "gray-feathered" in Greek.

BLUE-HEADED VIREO

(*Vireo solitarius*)

The bold eye-ring of the blue-headed vireo is quite apparent

This musically inclined bird was once lumped together with Cassin's and plumbeous vireos as a single species, the solitary vireo.

APPEARANCE

Length: 5.5 inches. *Wingspan:* 9.5 inches. Olive-green back, dull yellow wingbars with yellow edges on the feathers; blue-gray head with very conspicuous white spectacles around the eyes; black bill with a slightly hooked tip; throat, breast and belly are white with a yellow wash on the sides.

HABITAT
Preferred habitat is around openings in the canopy of coniferous and mixed coniferous-deciduous forests with mature trees and a shrubby understory. Is sometimes found in pure deciduous woodland.

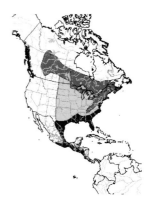

The range of the blue-headed vireo

BEHAVIOR
Forages mid-height in the forest, primarily by moving slowly while gleaning insects from twigs and foliage. Occasionally will capture insects in midair or pick them off leaves while hovering. This very tame, curious bird can be attracted to come very close by making the birder's *pish-pish-pish* sound. Flight is direct on rapidly beating wings.

CALLS
Song is similar to the red-eyed vireo's but higher in pitch and slower as well as more drawn out with longer intervals between phrases. Usually sings from high in the canopy. Call is a descending series of scolding, nasal chatters.

FOOD
Diet consists of primarily insects and caterpillars. Berries and fruit are also taken, especially in winter.

FAMILY LIFE
Monogamous pair; both sexes build a deep, cup-shaped nest of fine grasses, shredded bark, spider silk, lichen and plant fibers that is suspended by its rim in the fork of a twig in a conifer or deciduous tree well below the canopy. It is fearless of intruders in the vicinity of the nest. The typical clutch of 3 to 5 eggs is incubated by both the female and male. The altricial young remain in the nest for 12 to 14 days and are fed by both parents. One or 2 broods per year.

MIGRATION
Arrives on its spring breeding grounds from late April to late May. Fall migration is later than other vireos and occurs between late August and late October.

CONSERVATION CONCERNS
Species status in North America is *secure* in the United States and Canada with an increasing population. Habitat loss in its neotropical wintering grounds is a cause for concern.

RELATED SPECIES
It is 1 of 14 regularly occurring species of the *Vireonidae* family in North America. Cassin's and plumbeous vireos show the closest resemblance.

A blue-headed vireo

RED-EYED VIREO

(Vireo olivaceous)

Red-eyed vireos sing tirelessly in late spring and early summer

One of the most abundant woodland birds in North America, no deciduous forest would seem complete without the red-eyed vireo's jubilant song pouring forth from high within the canopy.

APPEARANCE
Length: 6 inches. *Wingspan:* 10 inches. Overall the bird has a sleek, smooth appearance. Olive green back and wings with no wingbars; gray crown, horizontal dark stripe passing through the eye, long whitish "eyebrow," and red eye (can be difficult to discern the color); long bill; underparts are whitish, occasionally with a faint green wash on the sides.

HABITAT
Deciduous and mixed woodlands, occasionally coniferous forests, forested suburbs and parks.

BEHAVIOR
Forages by gleaning insects from foliage and twigs. Often takes insects by hovering and picking them off leaves. The red-eyed vireo is somewhat slow moving as it goes about its daily business of feeding. The bird's most notable behavior is the male's prodigious singing during the breeding season. From a high perch it will often sing practically nonstop throughout daylight hours, and occasionally through the night. In flight it alternates quickly beating wings with short glides.

The range of the red-eyed vireo

CALLS
Its song is a seemingly endless series of short phrases, each one sharply separated from the next and sounding like *over-here, up in the tree, see-me-now, I see you*. One researcher counted over 22,000 such phrases in one single summer day! The call note is a whining, nasal *quee*.

FOOD
Diet consists largely of insects, caterpillars and spiders and other invertebrates such as snails. During fall migration and on wintering grounds its diet is mostly fruit and berries.

FAMILY LIFE
Monogamous pair; both sexes build a well-made, deeply cupped nest of soft plant fibers, shreds of bark, fine grasses, insect cocoons, lichens and spider silk suspended by the rim in the fork of a twig. The typical clutch of 3 to 5 eggs is incubated by the female for 11 to 14 days. Altricial young stay in the nest for 10 to 12 days and are fed by both parents. One or 2 broods per year.

A red-eyed vireo sings in a thicket

MIGRATION
Spring migrants generally arrive from early April to mid-May. Fall migration occurs from late August to early October.

CONSERVATION CONCERNS
Species status overall in North America is *secure* in the United States and Canada with an increasing population, particularly in the eastern part of the continent.

RELATED SPECIES
The red-eyed is 1 of 14 species of birds in North America belonging to the genus *Vireo*. The warbling, Philadelphia, black-whiskered and yellow-green are most similar to the red-eyed vireo.

YELLOW WARBLER
(*Dendroica petechia*)

The female yellow warbler lacks the bright yellow plumage and the orange breast accents of the male

The brightly colored yellow warbler is one of the most widespread species on the continent.

APPEARANCE
Length: 5 inches. Wingspan: 8 inches. Is the brightest yellow of all the warblers, slightly olive-yellow on top. The dark eyes contrast dramatically with the bright yellow face. The male has red or orange vertical streaks on its breast, and the female is similar except it is drabber and lacks streaks; slender black bill; the inner webs of the tail show large yellow patches that distinguish it from other warblers. Southern birds may have some orange or chestnut on the head.

HABITAT

Prefers moist areas with dense thickets of alders, willows, briars, and other vegetation in lowlands. Is at home in orchards, hedgerows, and shrubbery. Is partial to vegetation along the edges of wet areas such as streams and ponds.

The range of the yellow warbler

BEHAVIOR

Is quite noticeable as it forages on the stems and leaves of trees, bushes and briars, etc. It deftly makes its way among the foliage nabbing small caterpillars. Yellow warblers will often hawk insects by flying from a perch to snap them up in midair. The male tends to feed in higher, less dense vegetation than the female, perhaps to be more visible to other males that may enter its territory. Flight is fairly weak on fluttering wings alternated with brief periods of wings held against the body.

The yellow warbler is a bird of shrubby areas with small, dense tree growth

CALLS

The geographically variable song is a bright, somewhat slurred phrase *tsee-tsee-tsee-tsee-sitta-wee-tsee*. The call is a simple *chip*.

FOOD

Diet consists mainly of insects, caterpillars, insect eggs and spiders. Also consumes berries.

FAMILY LIFE

Monogamous pair; the female and male (mostly female) build a cup-shaped nest of grasses, weed stems, moss, lichen and spider's silk, lined with animal hair, downy plant matter and fine grasses. It is

A male yellow warbler moves through a thicket of wild roses

placed in the fork of a tree or bush, normally 3–13 feet high. The typical clutch of 3 to 6 eggs is incubated by the female for 11 or 12 days. The altricial young remain in the nest for 9 to 12 days and are fed by both parents. One or 2 broods per year.

MIGRATION
It normally arrives on its breeding grounds in late April to late May (earlier in more southerly areas of its range). Fall migration generally occurs from late July to early September and sometimes into October.

CONSERVATION CONCERNS
Species status overall in North America is *secure* in the United States and Canada. Population is declining in the southwestern United States where its preferred habitat of riparian woodlands is being destroyed at an alarming rate. Brown-headed cowbird brood parasitism is also widespread among this species. However, this extremely wide-ranging bird is still quite plentiful in its preferred habitat across North America.

RELATED SPECIES
It is part of the wood warbler family, which has 53 species in North America. Its genus, *Dendroica*, includes 20 other species, including the prairie warbler, Cape May warbler and magnolia warbler, all of which also show considerable yellow.

WILSON'S WARBLER

(*Wilsonia pusilla*)

A female Wilson's warbler in its typical habitat in a moist woodland

This warbler of wet northern and western forests is quite tame and is attracted to the *pish, pish, pish* call of birders.

APPEARANCE
Length: 4.75 inches. *Wingspan:* 7 inches. Is an overall greenish-yellow warbler with olive-green upperparts; bright yellow face; long tail appears darker than the body and is often raised. The male has a distinctive black cap. The female lacks the black cap, having a grayish wash on the crown instead. The bill is small and bristles at its base extend past the nostrils.

HABITAT

Prefers damp woodlands everywhere within its range—spruce forests of the east, the boreal forest of Alaska and northern Canada, bogs, fens and near streams and ponds. Is often found near willows and alders and other low shrubs. Has an extraordinary north to south breeding range from northern Alaska to southern California.

The range of the Wilson's warbler

BEHAVIOR

Is an extremely energetic forager. Usually stays within about 10 feet of the ground, and picks food off foliage by gleaning. Often hawks for insects, catching them in midair. Hovers while taking insects from foliage and twigs. Picks among the cracks and crevices of tree bark for food. The tail usually moves up and down as it feeds. Is very tame and easy to approach. Will usually respond quickly to birding calls. Flight, usually of short duration, is direct on rapidly beating wings.

CALLS

Song is a weak series of 10 or more rapidly repeated whistled notes, usually on the same pitch, *chi-chi-chi-chi*, generally dropping in pitch and either increasing or decreasing in volume toward the end. Call is a hard, nasal *chip*.

FOOD

Diet includes insects, insect larvae and eggs, spiders and other small invertebrates, and occasionally berries.

FAMILY LIFE

Monogamous pair; some populations are polygynous (male takes more than 1 mate). Female builds a cup-shaped nest of grass, moss, dried leaves, rootlets, with a lining of fine grass and hair that is placed on the ground and well hidden in a tussock of grass or moss, or occasionally placed near the ground in a low shrub. The typical

213

clutch of 4 to 6 eggs is incubated by the female for 10 to 13 days. Altricial young remain in the nest for 8 to 11 days and are fed by both parents. One brood per year.

MIGRATION
Spring migrants usually arrive on their breeding grounds between early March and late May. Fall migration generally occurs between mid-August and mid-October.

CONSERVATION CONCERNS
Species status overall in North America is *secure* in the United States and Canada. Recent declines have been noted in the western part of its range, possibly due to destruction of its breeding habitat.

RELATED SPECIES
A member of the large family *Parulidae*, which contains 53 species in North America. Is 1 of 3 warblers belonging to the genus *Wilsonia*, which also includes the hooded warbler and the Canada warbler.

The bold black cap of the male Wilson's warbler is unmistakable

NORTHERN PARULA

(Parula americana)

A male northern parula flitting about in the understory

The dainty northern parula, one of our smallest wood warblers, can be seen actively flitting about upper tree branches looking for insects in springtime.

APPEARANCE

Length: 4.5 inches. *Wingspan:* 7 inches. Is a very small, delicate bird; multicolored; top half is bluish gray with a greenish wash on the back, yellow throat and breast with a blue-gray head; white underparts; the male has dark rufous necklace on the top of the breast; the bill is dark above, orange below; 2 distinctive white wingbars and a distinctive white eye-ring.

HABITAT

Usually prefers moist deciduous, evergreen or mixed forests. Is also found near swamps, wetlands, streams or lakes. In the southern part of its range it is often found in deciduous bottomlands near swamps and rivers. Because abundant lichen or moss, such as beard moss in northern areas and Spanish moss in the South, is required for nesting, the parula is most often found in mature forests where these species thrive.

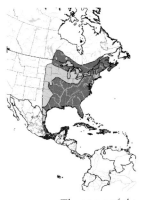

The range of the
northern parula

BEHAVIOR

Is very active, gleans insects from foliage, and is most often found in the mid to upper canopy, usually out of sight. It often hovers and hawks for insects. Will sometimes cling upside down on a branch in the manner of a chickadee. When encountered, parula tend to be somewhat tame and trusting compared to many woodland species. Flight is swift on rapidly beating wings.

One of the tiniest of the
warblers, a northern
parula perches on
a twig

CALLS

The male's song is a thin rising buzzing trill with an abrupt end note, *zzzzzzzz-zip* or altenatively, a series of buzzes, *zzz-zzz-zzz-zz*. Call is a sharp *tsip*.

FOOD

Insects, insect larva, small caterpillars and spiders.

FAMILY LIFE

The parula's breeding biology is poorly known because of the difficulty of observing its nest. The female builds a pendulum-shaped nest almost exclusively in a clump of "old man's beard" (usnea lichen) in the North or Spanish moss in southern areas. Occasionally it will build a nest in a tangled vine or clump of vegetation. The nest may be placed up to 55 feet off the ground and is lined with fine materials such as plant down. The typical clutch of 3 to 5 eggs is incubated mostly by the female for 12 to 14 days. The male will feed the female while she incubates. Altricial young remain in the nest for 10 or 11 days and are fed by both parents. Young stay in vicinity of the nest and remain dependent on parents for an undetermined period. One or 2 broods per year.

MIGRATION
Is one of the earliest spring migrants among warblers and usually arrives on its breeding ground in early to late May. Southerly migration generally peaks between September to mid-October.

CONSERVATION CONCERNS
Species status overall in North America is *secure* in the United States and Canada. However, it is endangered in Delaware and threatened in Massachussetts and Rhode Island. Deforestation on the Yucatan Peninsula of Mexico, a key wintering area for the parula, may have a significant impact on its population in the future.

RELATED SPECIES
Its closest relative is the rare tropical parula, which is restricted to a limited range in southern Texas.

A conservation status map of the northern parula

For many North American woodland birds that migrate to the neotropics (southern Mexico, Central and South America), the greatest threat to their survival is destruction of their wintering habitat. Many of the birds that are so familiar to us—such as warblers, flycatchers and vireos, to name but a few—must have quality habitats both in the North where they breed and in the South. The continued destruction of tropical forests is making it increasingly difficult for many species to survive the winter, so regardless of how well they are protected in the United States and Canada, we must ensure their well-being in the tropics if we wish to see them at home.

YELLOW-RUMPED WARBLER

(Dendroica coronata)

A male yellow-rumped warbler in breeding plumage on a tamarack tree

The yellow-rumped warbler's vast breeding range and wide variety of habitats has made it one of the most abundant wood warblers on the continent.

APPEARANCE

Length: 5.5 inches. *Wingspan:* 9 inches. Two variants exist—the western Audubon's warbler and the eastern myrtle warbler. The males of both are bluish-gray with black accents above, black on the face; 2 white wingbars; yellow sides; a white belly. The Audubon has a yellow throat and less white around the eye, while the myrtle warbler has a bright white throat and a distinctive white "eyebrow" and eye-ring. The females of both variants are similar to the males, but duller. All have a relatively long tail.

HABITAT

Lives in coniferous and mixed coniferous-deciduous forests, preferring open stands and the edges of clearings. Is found farther north than other warblers. During migration and when wintering it is a generalist that is found in practically any kind of habitat, including hedge and fence rows, garden shrubs, field edges and brushy tangles.

The range of the yellow-rumped warbler

BEHAVIOR

An active feeder that gleans insects from the ground and foliage, often hovering while it does so. It will frequently hawk insects by flying out from a perch and nabbing them in midair. Males usually forage higher up than females. Is occasionally seen skimming across the water picking up insects in the manner of a swallow. Will often congregate into flocks. Flight is quick on rapid wingbeats alternating with short periods of wings held against the body.

A female yellow-rumped warbler

CALLS
A slow trill of thin warbled notes usually rising or falling at the end, similar to the song of the dark-eyed junco. The call is a short *chip*.

FOOD
Eats insects, caterpillars and spiders. Unlike most warblers, a fair percentage of the yellow-rumped's diet consists of berries and seeds, which enables it to survive further north in winter than other warblers. It is one of the few warbler species that is occasionally seen at winter bird feeders.

FAMILY LIFE
The female builds a cup-shaped nest of twigs, rootlets, bits of bark and plant stalks lined with feathers, which is usually placed in an evergreen from ground level to 50 feet up. The typical clutch of 4 or 5 eggs is incubated by the female for 12 or 13 days. The young remain in the nest for 10 to 12 days and are fed by both parents. One or 2 broods per year.

MIGRATION
Usually arrives on breeding grounds from late April until mid-May. Though it departs some breeding areas as early as August, it is one of the last wood warblers to be seen in the fall, often lingering until December if a good supply of seeds or berries is available. Occasionally will overwinter successfully as far north as Nova Scotia.

CONSERVATION CONCERNS
Species status overall in North America is *secure* in the United States and Canada. Its continued abundance is likely the result of a huge breeding range and adaptability to several habitat types.

RELATED SPECIES
The Audubon's and myrtle variants of the yellow-rumped warbler were until relatively recently thought to be 2 separate species. Is 1 of the 21 members of the genus *Dendroica*.

MAGNOLIA WARBLER

(*Dendroica magnolia*)

A magnolia warbler enjoys a rain shower while perched in a spruce

With its highly visible yellow, black-and-white markings and brilliant song, the magnolia is unmistakable in its summer habitat across North America.

APPEARANCE

Length: 5 inches. *Wingspan:* 7.5 inches. The male has distinctive, bold plumage; black back; gray wings with heavy white markings; large, squared-off white patches on tail; gray head with white markings, black mask and yellow throat; underparts yellow with black streaks. The female lacks the white on the head and the black mask.

HABITAT
Inhabits open stands of small evergreens in spruce-fir-hemlock forest. Prefers dense young growth and is not often found far above the ground.

BEHAVIOR
This very active warbler gleans food from branches and foliage where it flits tirelessly from place to place, showing off its bold colors and flashing its striking black-and-white tail. Will sometimes capture flying insects by hawking them from a perch. Often sings its song while it forages. Flight is typical of warblers on fluttering wings, alternating with short periods of wings held against the body.

The range of the magnolia warbler

CALLS
The male's song is one of the most distinctive of the wood warblers, a sweet *weeta-weetah-weetee* or *weetah-weetah-weetoh*.

FOOD
Diet consists of insects, insect larva, caterpillars and spiders. Rarely eats berries or fruit.

FAMILY LIFE
Monogamous pair; both male and female build a loose cup-shaped nest of fine grass, small twigs and plant stems lined with tiny rootlets. Nest is built low in a spruce, fir or hemlock usually at a height of no more than 15 feet. The typical clutch of 4 eggs is incubated by the female for 11 to 13 days. The young remain in the nest for about 10 days and are fed by both parents. One brood per year.

A male magnolia warbler in full song

MIGRATION

Usually arrives on breeding grounds between late April and late May. Fall migration occurs from mid-August to early October.

CONSERVATION CONCERNS

A conservation status map of the magnolia warbler

Species status overall in North America is *secure* in the United States and Canada. It appears that populations may be increasing somewhat, at least in places, because forest clearing is creating the young, open undergrowth that the bird prefers for breeding. However, some populations in the southeastern United States, at the southern limit of the breeding range, are endangered.

RELATED SPECIES

It is 1 of the 21 species belonging to the *Dendroica* genus in North America, and the most similar in appearance (breeding males) to the yellow-rumped warbler.

ORANGE-CROWNED WARBLER

(Vermivora celata)

Despite its name, the orange on the orange-crowned warbler is virtually invisible

Despite its name, the orange crown of this common, widespread bird is rarely seen, usually becoming apparent only when the bird is under stress.

APPEARANCE
Length: 5 inches. *Wingspan:* 7.5 inches. Is a drab warbler with olive-green upperparts, faint streaking on sides and dull yellow underparts; no visible wingbars; the male and female are similar; orange crown is rarely visible.

HABITAT

Prefers thickets wherever it lives, brushy areas in deciduous woods and second growth in clearings or in burned-over areas. The low shrubbery and trees along streams, especially in deeply shaded areas, are a favorite haunt.

BEHAVIOR

Tends to be tame and curious, and is easily called in by using the birder's standard *pishing* sound. Less active than many other warblers, the orange-crowned is quite slow in its movements

The range of the orange-crowned warbler

as it searches along branches and among leaves for its insect prey. Forages generally in the lower parts of the woods. Is commonly observed eating sap from drill holes made by sapsuckers. Sometimes winters as far north as New England where it occasionally shows up at bird feeders.

An orange-crowned warbler foraging for insects

CALLS
The song is highly variable among individuals, but in general it is a short musical trill, beginning with slower notes, then quickening and rising toward the end. Call is a sharp *chip*.

FOOD
Diet consists mainly of insects, but also includes some berries as well as sap from sapsucker holes.

FAMILY LIFE
Monogamous pair; the female builds a cup-shaped nest on the ground under a bush, and rarely off the ground in a low shrub. Nest is constructed of coarse grasses, bark and leaves and lined with soft material. The typical clutch of 4 or 5 eggs is incubated by the female for 12 to 14 days. The young remain in the nest for 8 to 10 days and are fed by both adults. One brood per year.

MIGRATION
A fairly early spring migrant, it usually arrives on its breeding ground between late April to late May. Fall migration generally occurs between mid-August and October.

CONSERVATION CONCERNS
Species status overall in North America is *secure* in the United States and Canada. It is quite abundant in suitable habitat and has a broad breeding distribution and a tolerance of varying environments.

RELATED SPECIES
One of 8 warblers belonging to the genus *Vermivora*, which also includes the Nashville warbler, Tennessee warbler and the blue-winged warbler, among others.

BLACKPOLL WARBLER

(Dendroica striata)

*A female blackpoll warbler
on a black spruce*

Despite being quite common, relatively little is known about the blackpoll warbler due to its habit of nesting in the remote boreal forest.

APPEARANCE

Length: 5.5 inches. *Wingspan:* 9 inches. Is one of the larger wood warblers. Because of its black crown, white cheeks and light underparts, from a distance the male appears similar to the black-capped chickadee. Upperparts are gray with bold black stripes. Underparts are white with some black striping. The female appears slightly lighter overall with no black cap. Both sexes have white wingbars, thin bills, yellow legs and short tails.

HABITAT

Prefers dwarf spruces and firs of the northern boreal forest. At lower latitudes is often found in areas of higher elevation or where ocean winds have created stunted trees along the coast. During migration it is found in a variety of woodlands.

The range of the blackpoll warbler

BEHAVIOR

Is a large warbler, relatively sluggish, and slow in its feeding activities. Gleans insects from foliage, branches and twigs, spending the majority of its time on the inner portions of branches. Occasionally will hawk or hover for insects. Can be quite tame on breeding grounds. Flight is fast and direct on rapidly beating wings.

CALLS

The male's song is a series of 10 to 20 high-pitched (possibly the highest frequency of any warbler), staccato, monotone notes, loudest in the middle, *tzeet-tzeet-tzeet-tzeet-tzeet*. The call is a sharp *chip*.

FOOD

Eats a variety of insects, caterpillars, larvae and spiders, and occasionally seeds and fruit such as pokeberries.

FAMILY LIFE

Monogamous pair; the female builds a bulky cup-shaped nest of twigs, bark and dried grass placed against the trunk in a low, scrubby conifer, most often a spruce. When nesting in coastal areas, gull feathers are often used to cover and conceal the eggs. Nest height is usually between 2–30 feet. The typical clutch of 4 or 5 eggs is incubated by the female for 12 days. Young remain in the nest for 11 to 12 days, fed by both male and female. One or 2 broods per year.

VIREOS AND WARBLERS

MIGRATION
Most spring migrants arrive on their breeding grounds in late April to mid-May. Fall migration occurs between August and October, generally peaking in September. The blackpoll has the longest migration of any warbler, with some populations traveling 5,000 miles from Alaska to Brazil.

CONSERVATION CONCERNS
Species status overall in North America is *secure* in the United States and Canada with possible declines in the southern parts of its breeding range. Generally, its remote breeding habitat is little disturbed by human activities. However, degradation because of acid rain may be affecting its subalpine habitat in the more southerly part of its range.

RELATED SPECIES
The blackpoll warbler belongs to the large genus *Dendroica*, which includes 21 species of North American wood warblers.

A blackpoll warbler male on a coastal black spruce

BLACK-AND-WHITE WARBLER

(Mniotilta varia)

A striking black-and-white warbler on its breeding territory

This species is distinctive among warblers both for its striking plumage and as the only one that forages for its prey on the bark of trees.

APPEARANCE
Length: 5.25 inches. *Wingspan:* 8.25 inches. The breeding male's strongly streaked black-and-white plumage on the head, wings, back and breast is unmistakable. The female is similar, but with much lighter underparts that lack the heavy streaking. It appears more creamy gray overall than the male. Both sexes have a long bill with a slight downward curve.

HABITAT

Is found in a wide variety of habitats from mature mixed and deciduous forests to smaller second growth. Shows some preference for woods on slopes and in ravines.

BEHAVIOR

The most distinguishing behavior of the black-and-white warbler is its habit of creeping up and down the trunks and main branches of trees in a manner similar to nuthatches as it probes into crevices of the bark looking for insects and egg

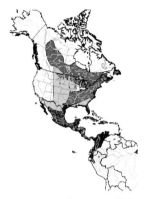

The range of the black-and-white warbler

masses to eat. It will also occasionally search for prey among the twigs and foliage and will hawk insects on the wing. Flight is somewhat undulating on rapid wing beats alternating with gliding with the wings pulled against the body.

CALLS

The male's song is a high-pitched series of double notes, the second being lower than the first, giving it a pleasant rolling effect, like the sound of a tiny squeaky wheel, *weesa-weesa-weesa-weesa-weesa.* The call is a hard *chip.*

FOOD

Eats insects, larvae, insect eggs, caterpillars and spiders. Unlike most other warblers, it does not eat fruit or berries.

FAMILY LIFE

Monogamous pair; the female builds a cup-shaped nest on the ground, usually near the base of a tree and well concealed by moss and dead leaves. Only rarely are nests placed above the ground. The typical clutch of 5 eggs is incubated by the female for about 10 days. Altricial young remain in the nest for 8 to 12 days and are fed by both parents. One or 2 broods per year.

Female black-and-white warblers are less dramatic than the males

MIGRATION

Because of its habit of foraging in the bark of trees for food, and less reliance on the presence of leaves, black-and-white warblers arrive earlier on their breeding grounds in spring than most warblers, usually from early April to mid-May. Fall migration generally occurs late August to October.

CONSERVATION CONCERNS

Species status overall in North America is *secure* in the United States and Canada with population apparently declining. Does not do well in smaller, fragmented woodlands, particularly areas with open forest canopies. Habitat destruction on its wintering grounds is also likely contributing to its apparent decline.

RELATED SPECIES

Although it is a member of the large avian family of *Parulidae*, the black-and-white warbler is the only member of the genus *Mniotilta*.

BLACK-THROATED GREEN WARBLER

(Dendroica virens)

A black-throated green warbler in a wet woodland

One of the most abundant breeding warblers of the Northeast, this highly vocal species makes its presence known by a persistent song that can be repeated hundreds of times per hour.

APPEARANCE
Length: 5 inches. *Wingspan:* 7.75 inches. The male has a moss-green back and crown; a black throat with a contrasting yellow face and white wingbars; white underparts with heavy black streaks on sides. The female is similar except the throat is mostly white.

HABITAT

Is a forest interior species that is intolerant of "patchy" or fragmented woodlands. Prefers open coniferous and mixed forest (particularly hemlock and white pine), especially where large trees are present. Is also attracted to bog communities of larch and spruce and coastal spruce forests. A southern subspecies, *Dendroica virens waynei*, lives in cypress swamps in the southeastern United States.

The range of the black-throated green warbler

BEHAVIOR

Spends much of its time at mid- to upper tree levels and is more often heard than seen. Is an active warbler that gleans insects from leaves and twigs and will often hunt them by hovering or by hawking. Males usually will feed higher in the trees than the females do. Flight is somewhat weak on fluttering wings alternating with glides with wings pulled against the sides.

CALLS

The male sings 2 songs: one is sung in the vicinity of its nest *zee-zee-zee-zoo-zee* and the other at the edge of its territory in interactions with other males *zoo-zee-zoo-zoo-zee*.

The call is a soft *tsip*.

FOOD

Eats largely insects, insect larvae, caterpillars and spiders. Will occasionally eat berries, especially on migration when insects are scarce.

Though one of the most commonly heard warblers, the black-throated green is not often seen due to its preference to be higher up in trees

A black-throated green warbler in a white pine

FAMILY LIFE

Monogamous pair; both sexes build a cup-shaped nest of grass, shreds of bark, small twigs and moss usually in the crotch of a small conifer from a few feet to 75 feet above the ground. The typical clutch of 3 to 5 eggs is incubated by the female for 12 days. The young remain in the nest for 8 to 10 days and are fed by both parents. One or 2 broods per year.

MIGRATION

Is an early spring migrant arriving on its breeding ground between late April and late May. Fall migration generally occurs through September and October.

CONSERVATION CONCERNS

Species status overall in North America is *secure* in the United States and Canada, but declining significantly in eastern North America. As a forest interior species, the black-throated green warbler often disappears from formerly contiguous woodland that has been cut up into smaller fragments. Loss of its wintering habitat in Central America, the Caribbean and Mexico may be impacting the population.

RELATED SPECIES

The black-throated green warbler is part of a widely distributed super-species group that includes the hermit, Townsend and golden-cheeked warblers (this last species is very similar in appearance to the black-throated green and is considered endangered).

CHESTNUT-SIDED WARBLER
(*Dendroica pensylvanica*)

A male chestnut-sided warbler in the spring woods

With its distinctive bright chestnut sides and pure white under-parts, the chestnut-sided warbler is one of the most easily recognizable of all North American wood warblers.

APPEARANCE

Length: 5 inches. *Wingspan:* 7.75 inches. Olive green upperparts with black streaking, yellow crown and black mask; the female has 2 black marks on the face, 1 behind and 1 in front of the eye; both male and female have chestnut-colored sides, though it is much more conspicuous on the male; underparts are pure white.

HABITAT

Prefers scrubby second-growth deciduous woods. Its ideal habitat is the brushy margins that sprout up after an area has been cut over and forest edges along open areas. Once younger trees get taller and a canopy is created over the woods, the chestnut-sided warbler becomes less common. This bird is rarely seen in mature forest. This species was extremely rare in the 1800s because of a lack of the suitable open habitat it prefers.

The range of the chestnut-sided warbler

BEHAVIOR

Forages by hopping and flying among the foliage, as it looks for insects, especially on the undersides of leaves. Tail is usually cocked high revealing bright white undertail feathers. Often forages on the ground and will also capture insects in flight and by hovering. During nesting season it will approach an intruder quite closely to attract attention away from the nest. Flight consists of fluttering wing beats alternating with short periods of gliding with wings against the body.

CALLS

The most common song, similar to the yellow warbler's, is a loud modulated phrase of *please-please-pleased to meetcha*, and is performed to establish a territory prior to nesting. The second song, which is less distinctive and lacks the strong up and down modulation of the first, is somewhat longer and rambling. Its call is a low *chip*.

FOOD

Diet consists of the usual warbler fare of insects, caterpillars and spiders, with a fair amount of berries taken when insects are scarce.

The male chestnut-sided warbler is one of the multicolored wood warblers

FAMILY LIFE
Monogamous pair; the female builds a loose cup-shaped nest of fine plant material, plant down, bark strips and vines lined with hair and rootlets. The typical clutch of 4 eggs is incubated by the female for 12 to 13 days. The altricial young remain in the nest for 10 to 12 days and are fed by both parents. One or 2 broods per year.

MIGRATION
Usually arrives on breeding grounds from late April to early May. Fall migration generally occurs between August and early October.

CONSERVATION CONCERNS
Species status overall in North America is *secure* in the United States and Canada. Chestnut-sided warblers are still widespread but declining. There is significant population reduction in the Adirondacks, northern New England and Nova Scotia. Threats include industrial logging, the loss of habitat to urbanization and the use of the biological control agent BT.

RELATED SPECIES
There are 20 other warbler species in North America belonging to the genus *Dendroica*.

BLACKBURNIAN WARBLER

(Dendroica fusca)

Blackburnian warblers are unmistakable with their orange plumage

Of all the wood warblers belonging to the large genus *Dendroica*, the colorful Blackburnian is the only species with bright orange plumage.

APPEARANCE

Length: 5 inches. *Wingspan:* 8.5 inches. The male has distinguishing flaming orange plumage over much of the front part of its body with a black back streaked in white; bold black mask and black accents down its throat and on its sides. A white wing panel is also unique to the male. The female has a subtler yellow wash with a tinge of orange and a less distinctive mask and white wingbars.

HABITAT

Tall trees in unfragmented forests of mature deciduous, mature coniferous or mixed forests, preferably with balsam fir, hemlocks, pines or spruces. Its favorite habitat is high among the upper branches of mature trees, well off the ground. Is found in a wider variety of habitats during migration.

BEHAVIOR

As with other wood warblers, the Blackburnian gleans insects, insect larvae and caterpillars from the foliage,

The range of the Blackburnian warbler

twigs and branches, usually very high up in trees. It will occasionally hawk for airborne insects by flying after them from a perch. Also captures prey by searching in the cracks and crevices of bark. Flight is fast and direct on rapidly beating wings.

CALLS

The song begins with four stronger double notes, followed by an ascending or descending series of thin notes, *tseep-tseep-tseep-tseep-titi-zeeeeee*. Call is a sharp *tsik*.

FOOD

Most important food items are caterpillars, insects and larvae. Will occasionally eat berries when primary food is scarce.

FAMILY LIFE

Monogamous pair; the female builds a cup-shaped nest high up in a conifer, usually on a branch some distance from the trunk. The typical clutch of 4 eggs is incubated by the female for 11 to 12 days. The altricial young remain in the nest for 9 to 12 days and are fed by both parents. One brood per year.

VIREOS AND WARBLERS

MIGRATION
Spring migrants usually arrive between late April and late May. Fall migration generally occurs between August and September.

CONSERVATION CONCERNS
Species status overall in North America is *secure* in the United States and Canada. The population is apparently increasing in Canada and is stable or decreasing in the United States. The Blackburnian warbler's need for mature forests puts it at odds with tree harvesting. This species does not do well in woodlands fragmented by logging or roads. The loss of broad-leafed woodlands in wintering areas in South America may have future impacts on the population.

RELATED SPECIES
A member of the large family *Parulidae*, which contains 53 species in North America, and the large 21-member genus *Dendroica*.

A male Blackburnian warbler in the understory

PALM WARBLER
(*Dendroica palmarum*)

A palm warbler in dull winter plumage

Despite its tropical sounding name, the palm warbler is one of the hardiest and most northerly breeding of the wood warblers. It is especially apparent in spring when it is often the first warbler to arrive in many areas.

APPEARANCE

Length: 5.5 inches. *Wingspan:* 8 inches. The male and female are similar. Is a drab warbler, overall brownish-gray above and pale yellow below; the brightest yellow is on the undertail feathers; rusty brown or rufous cap and a dark horizontal eye-line; faint brown streaking on breast. Most distinguishing characteristic is the continuous bobbing of its long tail.

HABITAT

Its summer haunts are in the North in open bogs and fens bordered by spruce, tamarack and balsam fir trees. In other seasons it is found in a wide variety of habitats, including in gardens, parks and hedgerows.

BEHAVIOR

Is the most ground-loving of the warblers in the genus *Dendroica*. Feeds primarily on the ground or in low bushes, particularly among fallen conifer cones. Also will hover occasion-

The range of the palm warbler

ally to glean food from vegetation and will sometimes catch insects in midair. Often feeds along the shores of lakes and ponds as it

migrates. Flight is weak with fluttering wings alternating with short periods of wings pulled against its body.

CALLS

The song is a rather weak, pleasant buzz or quick trill that is loudest in the middle, *swee-swee-swee-swee*. Sometimes there are a few tinkling notes at the end. The call is a strong *tsip*.

FOOD

Diet largely consists of insects, caterpillars and spiders, but can also occasionally include seeds and berries, such as bayberry.

A male palm warbler in breeding plumage

FAMILY LIFE

Monogamous pair; the female builds a cup-shaped nest of grass and shredded bark, usually in a bog on a hummock of sphagnum moss, but is occasionally built very low near the trunk of a spruce or sometimes in dry pine forests. The typical clutch of 4 to 5 eggs is incubated by the female for 12 days. The altricial young remain in the nest for 12 days and are fed by both adults. One brood per season.

MIGRATION

Is one of the earliest warblers to arrive on its breeding ground in the spring, showing up from mid-April to mid-May. Fall migration generally occurs from mid-September to late October.

CONSERVATION CONCERNS

Species status overall in North America is *apparently secure* in the United States and *secure* in Canada. Its status in the U.S. is due to a very restricted breeding range there. Very low population numbers in Vermont, New Hampshire and Michigan.

RELATED SPECIES

One of 21 warblers in the genus *Dendroica*.

NORTHERN WATERTHRUSH

(Seiurus noveboracensis)

A northern waterthrush with a bill full of insects

Despite its name, the northern waterthrush is actually a large warbler of northern forests, bogs and streams that is closely related to the ovenbird.

APPEARANCE
Length: 6 inches. *Wingspan:* 9.5 inches. Dark brown wings, back and crown; whitish or pale yellow undersides with dense vertical streaking; pale, narrow "eyebrow" and a sharp, pointed bill; relatively long legs for a warbler.

HABITAT
Lives near wooded swamps, shrubby bogs, lakes and slow-moving streams of northern and boreal coniferous and mixed forests.

BEHAVIOR

Forages largely on the ground (often wet areas at the edge of small water bodies) and low branches. Picks food from the mud and from under leaves and other detritus. Wades into shallow water to retrieve food on the surface. Occasionally hawks or hovers to capture flying insects. Bobs head and tilts tail repeatedly. Walks rather than hopping on the ground. Flight is swift with rapid wing beats.

The range of the northern waterthrush

CALLS

The song is a series of emphatic, short notes with a bubbling, liquid quality *seet-seet-swee-swee-swee-chew-chew-chew-chew*. The call is a sharp, steely *chink*.

FOOD

Terrestrial and aquatic insects, caterpillars and other invertebrates such as spiders, small crustaceans and mollusks. Occasionally takes small fish.

FAMILY LIFE

Monogamous pair; the female builds a cup-shaped nest of mostly moss, liverwort and a few leaves with an inner bowl of small twigs, tree needles, grass and rootlets and lined with mammal hair. Is usually hidden among the roots of a fallen tree in a wooded swamp, in clumps of ferns or under an overhanging stream bank. Typical clutch of 3 to 6 eggs is incubated by the female for 12 days. Altricial young remain in nest for about 10 days and are fed by both parents. One brood per year.

MIGRATION

Usually arrives on its northern breeding grounds between late April and late May. Fall migration generally occurs between early August and October.

CONSERVATION CONCERNS
Species status overall in North America is *secure* in the United States and Canada. Despite relatively low human disturbance of its summer breeding habitat, the mangrove forests it depends on in winter in Mexico, Central and South America and the West Indies are being destroyed at a rapid rate.

RELATED SPECIES
Is 1 of 3 species belonging to the genus *Seiurus* in North America. The other 2 are the Louisiana waterthrush and the ovenbird.

OVENBIRD
(Seiurus aurocapilla)

The ovenbird's bold eye-ring and rufous crown are visible here

Named for its oven-shaped nest, this somewhat drab and incon-spicuous species possesses one of the loudest songs relative to its size of any North American bird.

APPEARANCE
Length: 6 inches. *Wingspan:* 9.5 inches. Is heavy-bodied compared to many other warbler species; uniform olive-brown back, wings and face; pale orange crown bordered by lateral dark stripes; bold white eye-ring; underparts are white with conspicuous dark streaks; feet and legs are a fleshy pink.

HABITAT

Usually lives in mature deciduous forests with a closed canopy and occasionally in a mature mixed forest or pine forest. Appears to be most abundant in dry woods with a relatively open understory.

BEHAVIOR

Forages primarily on the ground where it walks among the leaf litter picking up insects. Occasionally it feeds in low bushes or saplings. Walks daintily with head bobbing and tail held high or wagging up and down. Sometimes will hover

The range of the ovenbird

or pounce on prey and only very rarely will it hawk for insects. Flight is low, rapid and steady on rapidly beating wings.

Spending most of its time on the forest floor or in the dense, low understory, the ovenbird is not often seen

CALLS

Most commonly heard song, performed from a low perch, is a loud *tee-cher, tee-cher, tee-cher* growing in volume toward the end. One bird's song will trigger another, then another until many ovenbirds are singing throughout the woodland. Two neighboring males may also sing their songs in perfect synchronization, one beginning seamlessly as the other leaves off, creating the impression that the original performer kept singing. A second song, uttered by the male in flight, is a complex jumble of warbling and twittering, usually with a few *tee-chers* added. Call is a sharp *chip*.

FOOD
Diet includes insects, insect larvae and eggs, spiders, snails, worms, berries, seeds and fruit.

FAMILY LIFE
Monogamous pair; the female builds a small, well-camouflaged, dome-shaped nest of dried leaves, grass, moss and plant fibers that is lined with hair and fine grass. The nest is placed on the ground among leaf litter and is entered through a hole in the side, hence the term "oven." The typical clutch of 4 or 5 eggs is incubated by the female for 11 to 14 days. The altricial young remain in the nest for 8 to 11 days and are fed by both parents. One or 2 broods per year.

MIGRATION
Most spring migrants arrive on their breeding grounds between late April and late May. Fall migration generally occurs from July to early October.

CONSERVATION CONCERNS
Species status overall in North America is *secure* in the United States and Canada. Population is increasing through much of its range.

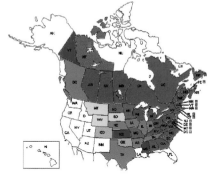

A conservation status map of the ovenbird

RELATED SPECIES
The ovenbird, along with the Louisiana waterthrush and the northern waterthrush, are the only North American warblers belonging to the genus *Seiurus*.

COMMON YELLOWTHROAT

(Geothlypis trichas)

A male common yellowthroat in full breeding plumage

Commonly seen in thickets and brushy areas, this colorful and inquisitive member of the warbler family is unmistakable in its bold yellow-and-black plumage.

APPEARANCE

Length: 5.25 inches. *Wingspan:* 7 inches. A small warbler, the male is a pale olive green on the upperparts and lower belly area with a bright yellow throat and a distinctive black mask; tail is rounded; bill is black and thin. The female is similar but lacks the black mask and is a little duller.

HABITAT

Inhabits dense woodlands and brushy areas in the vicinity of marshes, thickets along the edges of wet meadows and bogs, bushes and shrubs around clearings and willows. Prefers moist areas, but is found in drier places as well.

BEHAVIOR

Is very energetic. Feeds quite close to the ground, often concealed deep in the midst of vegetation. Flicks its tail and sometimes droops wings. Flits from plant to plant, climbing vertically up

The range of the common yellowthroat

and down stems, or hops on the ground as it gleans insects from leaves and grass. Occasionally catches insects in midair and sometimes hovers as it picks food from foliage or the ground. Flights tend to be short and jerky and usually just a few feet from one clump of vegetation to the next. The female is less often observed.

CALLS

The male's song, performed from a low perch, is a bright and rollicking *witchery-witchery-witchery-witch*, reminiscent of a squeaky wheel spinning. The song varies geographically. Also has a husky *tsip*, which it may repeat several times.

FOOD

A varied assortment of insects, larvae, spiders and seeds is taken.

FAMILY LIFE

Monogamous pair; a bulky nest of dead leaves and grasses is usually built by the female on the ground under a tangle of briars or other vegetation. The typical clutch of 3 to 5 eggs is incubated by the female for 12 days. Altricial young remain in the nest for 10 days and are fed by both parents. Two broods per year.

VIREOS AND WARBLERS

MIGRATION
Usually arrives on its breeding grounds in early April to late May (earlier in the South). Fall migration generally occurs from late August to late October.

CONSERVATION CONCERNS
Species status overall in North America is *secure* in the United States and Canada, although one survey has shown significant declines in parts of its range. Additionally, 2 sedentary populations, the salt marsh yellowthroat of California and the Brownsville yellowthroat of south Texas, have undergone drastic declines and may become extinct due to severe habitat loss.

RELATED SPECIES
A member of the warbler family, the common yellowthroat is the only species in its genus *Geothlypis*, but has up to 14 subspecies across North America.

A female common yellowthroat

AMERICAN REDSTART

(Setophaga ruticilla)

An American redstart male in breeding plumage

This common and highly animated wood warbler is known for its habit of drooping its wings slightly and fanning its long tail as it rests between bouts of flitting through the understory.

APPEARANCE

Length: 5.25 inches. *Wingspan:* 7.75 inches. The male is largely black on top with bright orange-red accents on the sides of the breast, wings and tail; light underparts. The female is olive gray above with gray undersides; yellow accents on side and tail. Both sexes have flattened bills and bristles around the mouth, and a long tail.

HABITAT

Favorite habitats are open deciduous and mixed woods, riparian areas, woodland edges, fence rows or open second growth. Prefers moist areas.

BEHAVIOR

The characteristic behavior of the redstart is its constant, energetic motion in pursuit of food. It is one of the most active and acrobatic of all the warblers as it flits about the branches. It's thought that the bird may flash its brilliant plumage to scare and flush prey from

The range of the American redstart

foliage. It gleans insects directly from leaves and twigs and captures them on the wing by darting from its perch. When perched, the bird will droop its wings and open and close them slightly, while spreading its tail. The male's black-and-orange plumage is unmistakable. Flight is somewhat undulating on fluttering wings alternating with gliding with wings pulled to the side of the body.

A female American redstart

CALLS
Its song is one of the loudest of the warblers. Although quite variable, it is generally a series of 4 or 5 loud notes ended by a loud *tzee-tzee-tzee-tzeo*. The call is a thin *tsip*.

FOOD
Diet consists of insects and insect larvae, caterpillars, spiders and rarely seeds or berries. Where their territories overlap, redstarts compete for the same food resource as the least flycatcher, which is a more aggressive species.

FAMILY LIFE
Monogamous pair; the female builds a cup-shaped nest of fine plant fibers, leaves, mosses and bits of bark and lichens that is often placed low in the fork of a tree, but also higher in larger trees, and only rarely on the ground. Will occasionally use old nests of other small woodland species. The typical clutch of 4 eggs is incubated by the female for 12 days. The altricial young remain in the nest for 9 days and are fed by both parents. One or 2 broods per year.

MIGRATION
Spring migration peaks in May. Fall migration generally occurs from late August to mid-October.

CONSERVATION CONCERNS
Species status overall in North America is *secure* in the United States and Canada, although local populations have declined in areas. Primary threat to the population is the degradation of its habitat through fragmentation, urbanization and development. As forests are fragmented there is increased nest parasitism by the brown-headed cowbird and nest predation by species such as blue jays and red squirrels.

RELATED SPECIES
Though a member of the large family *Parulidae*, the American redstart is the only member of the genus *Setophaga*.

Did You Know?

Just as we sometimes walk slowly or quickly, or break into a run, birds will fly only as fast as necessary given the circumstances in which they find themselves. In order to save precious energy, birds generally fly only as fast as they have to, particularly around their home territories. A warbler flitting from tree to tree in search of insects will fly at a slower pace than the same one migrating across the Gulf of Mexico. While peregrine falcons reach speeds in excess of 100 miles per hour while diving after prey, and eider ducks fly at 50 miles per hour, most small woodland birds fly only between 10 and 40 miles per hour.

BALTIMORE ORIOLE

(Icterus galbula)

A male Baltimore oriole in brilliant breeding-season plumage

Though a bird of forest edges, the Baltimore oriole has adapted well to urban parks and other human-altered landscapes.

APPEARANCE

Length: 8.75 inches. *Wingspan:* 11.5 inches. The male has a bright orange breast and belly, black head and back, orange-yellow shoulder patch and white wingbars. The female is duller overall without black accents.

HABITAT
Prefers woodlands in riparian areas, trees along roads, parkland and the edges of mature deciduous woodlands, often near human habitation. Is partial to elm trees in the East.

BEHAVIOR
Forages by gleaning food from branches and leaves, usually high in the trees. Will also hawk flying insects. Takes seeds at winter bird feeders and sips nectar from flowers in spring. Flight is direct on rapidly beating wings.

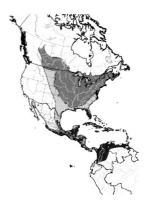

The range of the baltimore oriole

CALLS
The male's song is a series of clear 2-tone whistled notes, *tew-dee, tew-dee, tew-dee*, often mixed with single notes and long pauses. The call is a clear *hew-lee*.

FOOD
Diet consists largely of insects, caterpillars, larvae, berries, seeds and nectar.

FAMILY LIFE
Monogamous pair; the male and female build a hanging pendulum-shaped nest, finely woven from variety of materials including plant fibres, twine, horsehair and other fibrous items. The nest is usually near the end of a long drooping branch in a deciduous tree, rarely a conifer. The typical clutch of 4 or 5 eggs is incubated by the female for 12 to 14 days. Altricial young remain in the nest for 14 days and are fed by both parents. One brood per year.

MIGRATION
Usually arrives on spring breeding grounds from mid-April to late May. Fall migration generally occurs from early August to late September.

*A male
Baltimore oriole
in a blossoming
springtime tree*

CONSERVATION CONCERNS
Species status overall in North America is *secure* in the United States and Canada, but is possibly declining slightly in areas.

RELATED SPECIES
One of the 8 regularly occurring oriole species in North America. The Bullock's oriole is the most closely related to the Baltimore oriole, which at one time was thought to be the same species.

HOODED ORIOLE

(Icterus cucullatus)

A male hooded oriole

This active, colorful bird has seen its range expand northward as it ably adapts to treed suburbs and parks.

APPEARANCE
Length: 8 inches. *Wingspan:* 10.5 inches. Slender with a long tail, the males have a black back, tail and wings with bold white wing-bars; orange-yellow (breeding color) or yellow belly, breast, head and nape; bold black mask and throat; long and slightly down-curved bill. The female is a dull olive-yellow overall with medium gray wings and faint light wingbars.

HABITAT
Lives in riparian woodlands, parkland with scattered trees, palm groves, mesquite, deciduous woodland and residential shade trees. Is often found in areas of human habitation.

BEHAVIOR
Gleans insects from foliage and branches of trees, shrubs and bushes. Will feed at different levels in the trees, often high up in the canopy as its flits from limb to limb, sometimes hanging upside down as it forages. Uses its sharp bill to puncture the base of flowers to feed on nectar. Occasionally it will feed on the ground where it moves about by hopping. Flight is rapid and direct with steady, strong wing beats.

The range of the hooded oriole

CALLS
The song is a series of colorful warbling whistles with chattering notes mixed in, and the call is a high pitched *chit* or a series of high chattered notes.

FOOD
Diet consists of insects and insect larvae, small invertebrates such as spiders and nectar and fruit. Is attracted to hummingbird feeders.

FAMILY LIFE
Monogamous pair; the female builds a hanging nest of woven blades of grass, palm or yucca fibers, moss, lined with hair, grass, wool and feathers. Nest is usually placed high in a palm, yucca or palmetto, hanging from a twig or branch surrounded by foliage or Spanish moss. Sometimes the nest is woven into a bunch of Spanish moss. Typical clutch of 3 to 5 eggs is incubated by the female for 12 to 14 days. Altricial young remain in the nest for 14 days and are fed by both parents. Two or 3 broods per year.

MIGRATION

Some birds are year-round residents. Birds in the northern part of the range are more likely to be migratory, but travel only short distances. Birds that migrate usually arrive on their breeding grounds between mid-March to early April. Fall migration generally occurs from mid-August to late September.

CONSERVATION CONCERNS

Species status overall in North America is *secure*. Species range expanding northward somewhat as it adapts to treed residential areas, parks and ornamental palms. Declines in some parts of its range may be due to cowbird nest parasitism.

RELATED SPECIES

Is 1 of 8 regularly occurring orioles in North America, all belong to the genus *Icterus,* including the hooded, Baltimore, Bullock's, orchard, Scott's, Altamira, Audubon's and spot-breasted orioles.

SONG SPARROW

(Melospiza melodia)

A song sparrow sings in the spring foliage

This drab, inconspicuous little sparrow brings a measure of warmth to the early days of spring with its melodious song. It is one of the most widespread birds in North America.

APPEARANCE
Length: 6.25 inches. *Wingspan:* 8.25 inches. A stocky bird with a relatively long tail, it has a short, semiconical bill; heavily streaked in brown, especially on the underparts; brown and gray stripes on the crown and one broad stripe down each side of the front of the throat that enclose a small white patch; streaks on the breast converge to form a large dark spot in the middle of the breast; dull pinkish flesh-toned legs.

HABITAT

Is widespread across a number of habitat types—forest edges, roadsides, gardens, bushy margins of marshes, lakes, wet meadows, alder thickets and other bodies of water. Is also found in upland areas near salt marshes.

The range of the song sparrow

BEHAVIOR

Forages by scratching the ground to get at seeds. Also gleans food from low trees, bushes and grass. Flies low on rapidly beating wings no more than 6–10 feet from the ground. Males are highly territorial during the breeding season and often engage in chases.

CALLS

The hallmark of the song sparrow is its beautiful territorial singing, which is heard primarily during the spring (but also later in the summer for a time). This spectacular song, which is performed from a series of perches around its territory, is complex and varied.

A song sparrow perches on a stump chewed by a beaver

It usually begins with 2 or 3 clear whistled notes followed by a varied trill. Also has a simple, single *tsimp* and *tseet*.

FOOD

Eats insects, spiders, larvae, seeds, berries and tiny crustaceans, as well as mollusks in coastal areas.

FAMILY LIFE

Monogamous pair; the female builds a small cup-shaped nest of grass, leaves and strips of bark, lined with soft materials such as fine grass and cattail down, which is placed on the ground beneath a low bush, brush pile or shrub. The typical clutch of 3 or 4 eggs is incubated by the female for 12 to 14 days. Altricial young remain in the nest for 9 to 16 days and are fed by both parents. Two or 3 broods per year.

MIGRATION
Most of the birds in the northern third of the range are migratory. It generally arrives on breeding grounds in March or April and leaves by late October in most places. Individuals often overwinter, even in the northern part of the range, in part relying on bird feeders.

CONSERVATION CONCERNS
Species status overall in North America is *secure* in the United States and Canada. The subspecies *graminea* of Santa Barbara Island, California, became extinct after introduced rabbits destroyed its habitat.

RELATED SPECIES
There are about 30 subspecies of song sparrows in North America. Two separate species, the swamp sparrow and Lincoln's sparrow both belong to the same genus, *Melospiza*.

Did You Know?

Some species of birds do not build nests or take care of their own young, but instead lay their eggs in other species' nests. In North America, the brown-headed cowbird lays its eggs in the nests of over 200 other species. Some of them, such as thrashers, robins and jays among others, will try to remove the cowbird's egg from the nest. Smaller species, such as many warblers, sparrows, vireos and phoebes, accept the cowbird egg, perhaps because they are too large to remove. Unfortunately, the cowbird egg usually hatches first and the young cowbird grows at a rapid rate, taking the food meant for the host's young, starving them in the process. Cowbird brood-parasitism has become a serious conservation problem as the continuing fragmentation of forests has led to easier access for cowbirds to the nests of traditionally interior forest nesting species. This is having a deleterious effect on the populations of many species of songbirds.

LINCOLN'S SPARROW

(Melospiza lincolnii)

A Lincoln's sparrow perched in the evening sunlight

This skulking, secretive bird of boreal bogs and thickets is one of the less commonly observed of North America's sparrow species and is relatively unknown from a scientific standpoint.

APPEARANCE

Length: 5.75 inches. *Wingspan:* 7.5 inches. Smaller and grayer than the familiar song sparrow, its back and wings are buff-colored and brown with dark streaks; top of the head is brown with black streaks divided by a gray band; side of the head is gray with a brown stripe running behind the eye, and a buff-color eye-ring; buff-brown breast band with fine dark striping and a light belly.

HABITAT

Inhabits subarctic and subalpine thickets and woodlands around fens, bogs, wet meadows, streams, ponds and swamps. Alders, willows, tamarack and spruce and dense ground vegetation are preferred. Is also found in mountain meadows in the West.

The range of the Lincoln's sparrow

BEHAVIOR

A very shy, secretive bird that spends most of its time on the ground skulking in dense bushy and shrubby areas. Forages largely on the ground using the typical "double-scratching" technique where it hops and rakes backward through the leaf litter to uncover food. Stops singing immediately on the approach of an intruder, flitting from spot to spot while incessantly chipping. Raises a small crest on its head when alarmed. Often migrates with other sparrow species. Flight is undulating with alternating rapid flapping and gliding.

SPARROWS

A Lincoln's sparrow with a nice juicy caterpillar for its young

CALLS

Its wren-like song is a short, hurried melody of liquid, musical trills, and somewhat buzzy notes that become higher in pitch and louder toward the end. Males generally possess a repertoire of two to four songs. The call is a *chep*. A second call, used in flight, is a thin *zeet*.

FOOD

Diet consists of seeds of trees, grasses and weeds, grains and insects, caterpillars, millipedes, spiders and other invertebrates. Will visit bird feeders during migration.

FAMILY LIFE

Monogamous pair; the female builds a cup-shaped nest of grass and fine sedges on the ground in a depression of moss or grass or on a tussock in a swampy area. The typical clutch of 4 or 5 eggs is incubated by the female for 12 to 14 days. Altricial young remain in the nest for 9 to 12 days and are fed by both sexes. One or 2 broods per year.

MIGRATION

Birds generally arrive on their breeding grounds between mid-April and late May. Fall migration usually occurs from early September to late October.

CONSERVATION CONCERNS

Species status overall in North America is *secure* in the United States and Canada. Breeding populations are affected by the herbicide spraying of the forest products industry. Populations in Quebec and other northern spruce-hardwood forests have experienced significant declines.

RELATED SPECIES

Lincoln's sparrow is a member of the very large sparrow family *Emberizidae* in North America. The song sparrow and swamp sparrow both belong to the same genus *Melospiza*.

FOX SPARROW

(Passerella iliaca)

A fox sparrow showing its red fox-colored plumage

The largest member of its family in North America, the fox sparrow possesses one of the most beautiful voices of the northern forest.

APPEARANCE

Length: 7 inches. *Wingspan:* 10.5 inches. Typically husky in appearance like other sparrows, the fox sparrow is so named for its distinctive plumage that is the color of a red fox; tail, back and wings are rufous; head is rufous and gray; underparts are white with bold rufous streaks converging in a large spot on the breast. The more northerly birds have the brightest plumage.

HABITAT

Lives in coniferous and mixed conifer-ous-deciduous forest undergrowth, northern taiga and subalpine forest, riparian willow and alder thickets, montane thickets, burned-over lands, regenerating clear-cuts and woodland edges and clearings.

The range of the fox sparrow

BEHAVIOR

Forages in typical sparrow fashion by scratching at the ground by hopping and pulling both feet backward at the same time, exposing insects and seeds in the leaf litter and humus. Also gleans food from foliage and branches. Is wary of humans. Male fox sparrows show aggression toward other species on breeding territory. Occasionally they are found in the company of other sparrow species during the non-breeding season. Flight is somewhat undulating with alternating flapping and gliding with wings held against the body.

CALLS

Song is rich and melodic. Each male possesses a repertoire of low warbling, lilting songs, and we could do no better than to quote Thoreau for an example of one of the most commonly heard ones: "I heard their loud, sweet, canary-like whistle thirty of forty rods off, sounding richer than anything yet; some on the bushes singing, *twee twee twa twa ter tweer tweer twa....*" Songs vary by geographical location. Eastern and northern populations have a smaller repertoire than western ones. Call is a *chip.*

FOOD

Takes a wide variety of food, including seeds, berries, buds, insects, spiders and other invertebrates.

FAMILY LIFE

Monogamous pair; the female builds a cup-shaped nest of lichens, grass, rootlets, leaves, feathers, animal hair and pieces of bark, lined with moss, grass and animal hair. It is placed on the ground or in a low shrub, rarely on the branch of a tree. Earlier nests are placed higher off the ground, perhaps due to snow. The typical clutch of 2 to 5 eggs is incubated by the female for 12 to 14 days. Altricial young remain in the nest for 9 to 11 days and are fed by both parents. Two broods per year.

A fox sparrow prepares to sing

MIGRATION

Although there are variations of migration timing for the 4 distinct geographical subspecies groups on the continent, birds generally arrive on their breeding grounds from early March to late April. Fall migration usually occurs from late August through September.

CONSERVATION CONCERNS

Species status overall in North America is *secure* in the United States and Canada.

RELATED SPECIES

One of the most geographically variable of North American songbirds, the fox sparrow has 18 recognized subspecies that belong to 4 distinct groups: the red fox sparrow from northern Alaska across the north to the island of Newfoundland; the slate-colored fox sparrow of the western interior mountains; the sooty fox sparrow of coastal Alaska and British Columbia; and the large-billed fox sparrow of Oregon and California. Recent genetic evidence suggests that the fox sparrow's closest species relative is the American tree sparrow, which is in a separate genus.

AMERICAN TREE SPARROW

(Spizella arborea)

An American tree sparrow feeding on the ground

This inconspicuous sparrow of the northern wilderness is seldom seen, except when it migrates south into settled areas in winter.

APPEARANCE
Length: 6.25 inches. *Wingspan:* 9.5 inches. Has a typical husky sparrow profile; wings are reddish brown with dark streaking and white wingbars; gray head with rufous crown and rufous line behind eye; long tail; 2-toned bill is dark on top and yellow below; underparts are grayish brown with rufous areas on flanks, sides and the sides of breast; dark central breast spot.

HABITAT

Breeding habitat includes taiga areas with scattered stunted trees and shrubs along the edge of the tundra, on the tundra itself, north of the treeline, along northern coasts in scrubby woods and in alders and willow along northern streams. In winter, it is found in mixed coniferous-deciduous woods, old fields and edge habitat next to woodland and often at feeders.

The range of the American tree sparrow

BEHAVIOR

Forages by using a typical sparrow double-scratch by hopping and pulling both feet backward at the same time, exposing insects and seeds on the ground. Also gleans food from foliage and twigs. Often jumps up from the ground to grab seeds from low branches or flits among tall weeds picking seeds. In winter it is often seen in the company of dark-eyed juncos. Flights are usually short and undulating with alternating flapping and gliding with wings held against the sides.

CALLS

Song is a sweet, varying warble *tsee-tsee-sweeeee-swee-swee-swee-swit-swit-swit*. Calls are a short, rolling *teel-wit, teel-wit* and a *tseet*.

FOOD

Eats mostly seeds and buds. During the breeding season insects, insect larvae, caterpillars and spiders and other small invertebrates are also taken.

FAMILY LIFE

Monogamous pair; the female builds a cup-shaped nest of grass, moss, bark strips and rootlets, lined with feathers, animal hair and fur. It is placed on the ground in a tussock of grass or moss, rarely in a low shrub or tree. The typical clutch of 3 to 5 eggs is incubated by the female for 12 or 13 days. Altricial young remain in the nest for 8 to 10 days and are fed by both parents. One brood per year.

MIGRATION
Spring birds arrive on their northern breeding grounds from late March to late May. Fall migration generally occurs from early September to October. It winters across southern Canada and most of the United States.

CONSERVATION CONCERNS
Species status overall for North America is *secure* in the United States and Canada. The fact that this species breeds largely north of areas of usable timber means that it hasn't been affected by human development to any great extent. However, large megaprojects, such as gas and oil, mining and hydroelectricity, could have a serious impact in the future.

RELATED SPECIES
It is 1 of 5 sparrows in North America that belong to the genus *Spizella*. Most similar in appearance is the field sparrow, *Spizella pusilla*.

*An American tree sparrow
in winter*

WHITE-THROATED SPARROW

(*Zonotrichia albicollis*)

White-throated sparrows sport bold yellow lores

The white-throated sparrow's often-heard unforgettable song is synonymous with northern woodlands.

APPEARANCE

Length: 6.5 inches. *Wingspan:* 9.25 inches. A large sparrow, quite similar to the white-crowned sparrow, with rufous brown upperparts with dark streaking and 2 white-wingbars; light brown rump; conspicuous dark brown stripes on head with bold white "eyebrows" and crown stripe; black stripe behind the eye; yellow spot in front of eyes; dark bill; bright white throat. A second color morph has tan head stripes rather than white. Underparts are gray.

HABITAT

Inhabits coniferous and mixed coniferous-deciduous forests, woodland edges and clearings such as regenerating clearcuts and thickets. One is likely to find a white-throated sparrow in the northern woods wherever openings have allowed the growth of brushy shrubs.

BEHAVIOR

Scratches among the leaf litter on the ground for food. Also gleans food from foliage and branches and hawks insects in midair. Travels in mixed flocks with

The range of the white-throated sparrow

other sparrow species in winter. Is somewhat shy, but can be easily attracted by a birder's *pishing* sound. Flight is undulating with rapidly beating wings alternating with short periods of wings held against the body. Is common at winter bird feeders.

CALLS

Its song is one of the most distinctive and easy to remember of North American woodland birds. A series of clear whistled notes, its sound has been variously interpreted as *pure-sweet-canada-canada-canada* or *old-sam-peabody-peabody-peabody*. There is significant variation between different populations and different ages of birds. It sometimes sings at night during breeding season. Calls are a metallic *tink* and a high *tseet*.

FOOD

Diet is mostly weeds, grass and tree seeds, buds, berries and fruits. Insects, caterpillars, spiders and other invertebrates are also taken.

FAMILY LIFE

Monogamous pair; the female builds a cup-shaped nest of twigs, pine needles, grass, wood chips and rootlets lined with fine materials. It is placed on or just above the ground in a shrub, well concealed and usually near the edge of a clearing. The typical clutch of 4 to 6 eggs

The lovely white-throated sparrow's appearance is as striking as its distinctive song

is incubated by the female for 11 to 14 days. Altricial young remain in the nest for 7 to 12 days and are fed by both parents. One or 2 broods per year.

MIGRATION
Birds generally arrive on their breeding grounds between late March and mid-May. Fall migration usually occurs from September to mid-November.

CONSERVATION CONCERNS
Species status overall in North America is *secure* in the United States and Canada.

RELATED SPECIES
White-crowned sparrow, Harris's sparrow and the golden-crowned sparrow, all of which have prominent crown stripes, belong to the same genus, *Zonotrichia*.

WHITE-CROWNED SPARROW

(Zonotrichia leucophrys)

The white-crowned sparrow is one of the widest ranging songbirds in North America

It is one of the most studied of all songbirds because of its relative abundance, wide distribution and easily observed behavior.

APPEARANCE

Length: 7 inches. *Wingspan:* 9.5 inches. Brown upperparts with dark streaking and 2 white-wingbars; light brown rump; white crown with conspicuous black stripes; black stripe behind the eye; orange bill; gray underparts.

HABITAT

Inhabits woody thickets of shrubs in open grassy areas such as tundra, beside streams and bogs in willow and dwarf birch, wet meadows and coastal windswept scrub woodlands. It also lives in brushy margins of open areas, chaparral and parkland during migration.

The range of the white-crowned sparrow

BEHAVIOR

Forages mostly by hopping and scratching at the ground for food like other sparrows. Also finds food in low shrubs and trees and will occasionally hawk for insects in flight. Occurs in flocks of 10 to 50 birds in winter that show a strong attachment to a given territory. Flight is slightly undulating with alternating flapping and gliding with wings pulled against the body.

CALLS

The song is a relatively brief 5- or 6-note long series of whistles, followed by buzzy, modulated trills sung from exposed perches. Its song sounds somewhat similar to but less melodic than that of the white-throated sparrow. The call is a sharp *tink* and a thin *tseek*.

FOOD

Diet includes seeds, berries, buds, insects, caterpillars and other invertebrates. Animal-based food is more important in spring and summer months.

FAMILY LIFE

Monogamous pair; some males mate with more than 1 female. Female builds a cup-shaped nest of grass, rootlets, twigs, shredded bark and leaves lined with feathers, animal hair and fine grass. The nest is placed on the ground in the grass or in a low shrub. The typical clutch of 3 to 5 eggs is incubated by the female for 11 to 14 days. Altricial young remain in the nest for 7 to 12 days and are fed by both parents. The male continues to feed young while the female begins a second nest. Two to 4 broods per year.

MIGRATION
Some populations are year-round residents. Birds that migrate generally arrive on their breeding grounds between late March and mid-May. Fall migration usually occurs between mid-August and early October.

CONSERVATION CONCERNS
Species status overall for North America is *secure* in the United States and Canada.

RELATED SPECIES
The white-throated sparrow, Harris's sparrow and the golden-crowned sparrow belong to the same genus, *Zonotrichia*.

A male white-crowned sparrow

DARK-EYED JUNCO

(Junco hyemalis)

The red-backed variation of the abundant dark-eyed junco

This rather shy little member of the sparrow family is one of the most widespread songbirds in North America, ranging from Alaska to Mexico.

APPEARANCE

Length: 6.25 inches. *Wingspan:* 9.25 inches. The most widespread of the subspecies of juncos, is the slate-colored. The male is generally a solid dark gray above, including head, throat and breast, with a white belly. The females tend to be slightly lighter overall, often with a tinge of brown on the head or back. Both sexes have pale, cream-colored bills and white outer tail feathers, which are especially apparent in flight. Another variation within the slate-colored race has much more brown on its back and flanks.

HABITAT

Lives in deciduous, coniferous and mixed forests particularly near edges, open woodlands, bogs, rural roadsides and in the vicinity of farms. In winter they are common around human habitations, particularly near the edges of woods and brushy areas. Is a very common feeder visitor.

The range of the dark-eyed junco

BEHAVIOR

Forages by gleaning insects from branches, foliage and plants and by hopping along and scratching at the ground for seeds. Occasionally hawks for insects. In the fall and spring will often forage in mixed flocks with chickadees, nuthatches, kinglets and sparrows. In winter, forms small flocks of 10 to 30 birds. The birds in these flocks are part of a social hierarchy. Flight is undulating with rapid wing beats alternating with brief periods of gliding with the wings pulled against the body.

A slate colored dark-eyed junco, the most common color variation of the species

CALLS

The male's song is a short, sweet, trill of a single tone. The call is a very hard, sharp *chip*, almost metallic in tone.

FOOD

Eats insects, caterpillars, spiders, grains, seeds and berries.

FAMILY LIFE

Monogamous pair; the male and female build a nest of grass, leaves, moss and bark on the ground, well concealed and often against a vertical surface, sheltered by bushes, shrubbery or a fallen tree. The typi-

This gray-headed junco is another geographical variation of the dark-eyed junco

cal clutch of 3 to 6 eggs is incubated by the female for 12 or 13 days. The young remain in the nest for 9 to 13 days and are fed by both parents. One to 3 broods per year.

MIGRATION
Spring migrants arrive on their breeding ground from April to June. Fall migration generally occurs between September and November.

CONSERVATION CONCERNS
Overall status in North America is *secure* in the United States and Canada. Is one of the most abundant birds on the continent, with a population estimated at over 600 million.

RELATED SPECIES
There are 5 subspecies that belong to the dark-eyed junco species, including the slate-colored, gray-headed, Oregon, pink-sided and white-winged juncos. The yellow-eyed junco is a separate (but very similar) species of the southwestern United States.

YELLOW-EYED JUNCO

(Junco phaeonotus)

The eyes of the yellow-eyed junco give the species a rather fierce appearance

Though limited in range, the yellow-eyed junco is a common bird around picnic sites and campgrounds in southeastern Arizona and southwestern New Mexico.

APPEARANCE

Length: 6.25 inches. *Wingspan:* 9.5 inches. Is similar in size and shape to the more widespread dark-eyed junco; medium gray with a reddish brown "saddle" above and light gray below; striking yellow eye with a partial dark mask; black upper mandible and yellow lower mandible; outer tail feathers are white like the dark-eyed junco.

HABITAT
Prefers open coniferous forest such as pine-oak woodlands in the transition and boreal elevation zones of the southwest. Is also found in brushy areas.

BEHAVIOR
Like its dark-eyed cousin, the yellow-eyed junco feeds primarily on the ground by scratching for seeds and gleaning insects from vegetation. Is quite tame and territorial. Will fight other male intruders with great vigor.

The range of the yellow-eyed junco

CALLS
The male's song is much more varied and warbler-like than the dark-eyed junco's and is made up of various trills and notes. The call is a sharp *tsip*.

FOOD
Eats insects, caterpillars, grains and seeds.

A yellow-eyed junco

FAMILY LIFE
Monogamous pair; the male and female build a nest on the ground of grasses and moss, lined with fine materials, occasionally up to 15 feet up in a tree. The usual 3 or 4 eggs are incubated by the female for 15 days. The altricial young remain in the nest for 10 days and are fed by both parents. Parents will evict the young from the breeding territory after about 28 days. Up to 3 broods per year.

MIGRATION
Nonmigratory resident but will move to lower elevations during cold weather.

CONSERVATION CONCERNS
Species status overall in North America is *vulnerable* due to its extremely limited range in the United States. Is threatened by destruction of mature deciduous woodlands.

RELATED SPECIES
The only other member of the *Junco* genus in North America is the widespread dark-eyed junco.

HOUSE FINCH

(Carpodacus mexicanus)

A male house finch

Historically found only in the western half of the continent, the house finch's range has expanded to include much of the eastern side of North America since it was introduced on Long Island, New York, in 1940.

APPEARANCE

Length: 6 inches. *Wingspan:* 9.5 inches. Is similar to the purple finch, but the male is less red and the female less streaked overall. The male has a brown back with faint streaking; brown cap; bright red face with pale gray cheek; red throat and breast. The female is overall gray-brown with streaks; short, rounded bill; whitish underparts with streaks; long tail.

HABITAT

A wide variety of semiopen or open habitat, including woodlands, parks and residential areas with some trees, arid scrubland, edges of agricultural fields, brushy areas and urban environments. Has adapted well to human-altered landscapes.

The range of the house finch

BEHAVIOR

Forages on the ground and in foliage; also picks buds off trees. Often clings to the heads of weedy plants to gather seeds. Drinks the sap of maple trees. Is highly gregarious, especially in winter when it is found in flocks at feeders and will roost in large aggregations. Mixes with other finch species outside of the breeding season. Flight is undulating with alternating flapping and gliding with wings held against the body.

CALLS

The song is a spirited, rolling warble of short phrases, varying in pitch and ending in low buzzy notes, somewhat similar to the purple finch. The call is a chirping *chi-weet*.

The female house finch is somewhat drab compared to her mate

FOOD

Diet consists almost exclusively of plant-based food such as seeds, buds, berries, fruit and maple sap. Insects are rarely taken.

FAMILY LIFE

Monogamous pair; often nests in loose colonies. The female builds a cup-shaped nest of twigs, grass, rootlets, feathers and small debris. Also appropriates nests abandoned by other species and will nest in cavities such as tree holes, bird boxes or under the eaves of buildings. The typical clutch of 4 or 5 eggs is incubated by the female for 12 to 14 days. Altricial young remain in the nest for 11 to 19 days and are fed by both parents. One to 3 broods per year.

MIGRATION

Year-round resident.

CONSERVATION CONCERNS

Species status overall in North America is *secure* in the United States and Canada. Is abundant throughout its range. Continent-wide population estimates range from almost 300 million to nearly 1.5 billion birds.

RELATED SPECIES

The house finch shares the genus *Carpodacus* with the purple finch and Cassin's finch.

PURPLE FINCH
(*Carpodacus purpureus*)

A male purple finch showing its "raspberry juice" plumage

This northern counterpart to the house finch is one of our most delightful species, with its lovely mellow warbling song and its "dipped in raspberry juice" plumage.

APPEARANCE

Length: 6 inches. *Wingspan:* 10 inches. The male is a rosy-red overall with raspberry-red head, reddish wings, red sides and breast; fairly apparent brown streaking on the back; white belly. The female is sparrow-like in appearance and has a brown back and wings with light streaks; whitish breast and belly heavily accented with dark streaking; white "eyebrow." Both sexes have deeply notched tails and a triangular bill.

HABITAT
Prefers open, moist coniferous forest, mixed forest, openings in the forest created by bogs, streams and ponds. Is also found in parks planted with an abundance of conifers.

The range of the purple finch

BEHAVIOR
Generally forages by gleaning buds and seeds toward the outer edges of branches. Occasionally will hawk by sallying from branches to capture slow-flying insects such as winged ants. Will extract nectar from flowers by crushing the calyx (the lowermost part of the flower) while leaving the rest intact. Will sometimes feed on the ground. Flight is distinctly undulating like a goldfinch. In winter it flocks with pine siskins and American goldfinches.

CALLS
Both sexes sing a long, bubbling, ascending warble that usually ends with a descending trill. In early spring the males may sing in chorus. Calls are a metallic *pick* and or melodic *wee-yu*.

FOOD
Eats seeds almost exclusively, but also buds, nectar and blossoms. In spring it will eat insects and in summer, berries.

FAMILY LIFE
Monogamous pair; the female builds a cup-shaped nest of twigs, grass, rootlets and bark strips in a branch or tree fork ranging from near ground level to 30 feet high. The typical clutch of 4 or 5 eggs is incubated by the female for 13 days. The young remain in the nest for 14 days and are fed by both adults. One or 2 broods per year.

MIGRATION

The southern portion of the population is nonmigratory. The rest of the population's migration times are highly variable, depending on the location. Migrants arrive on breeding grounds between February and May. Fall migration occurs between late August and December. The purple finch is noted for periodic irruptions throughout the northern part of its range and numbers can increase dramatically where there is a bumper crop of conifer cones.

CONSERVATION CONCERNS

Species status overall in North America is *secure* in the United States and Canada. A decline has been observed in the eastern United States, where the purple finch may be outcompeted by the introduced house finch. Although small-scale logging can actually result in the open woodland habitat preferred by the species, industrial clear-cut logging on its breeding grounds may be detrimental to the species.

RELATED SPECIES

The purple finch is 1 of 3 species in North America that belong to the genus *Carpodacus*. The other 2 are the house finch and the Cassin's finch.

A male purple finch

COMMON REDPOLL

(Carduelis flammea)

A common redpoll in flight in the falling snow

One of the most widespread birds in the northern hemisphere, this diminutive Arctic-breeding finch is found in northern North America, Asia and Europe.

APPEARANCE

Length: 5.25 inches. *Wingspan:* 9 inches. Is virtually the same size as the American goldfinch. Upperparts are whitish with dark streaking; red or orange-red cap; black chin; sharp, short, yellow conical bill; heavy dark streaking on flanks. Males have a rose-pink breast.

HABITAT

Breeding habitat includes subarctic and boreal forest openings, willow, alder and tamarack swamps. In winter they may move southward where they inhabit a variety of wooded and open habitats.

The range of the common redpoll

BEHAVIOR

Is almost always found in flocks, and is an acrobatic forager that flits from place to place where it spends as much time hanging upside down from the tips of twigs and weeds in pursuit of food as it spends right-side up. Also forages on the ground. Feeding is accompanied by incessant chattering. Is very tame and approachable. Flight is undulating with alternating flapping and gliding with wings held against the body. Calls while in flight.

CALLS

The song is a series of short, rippling trills, twitters, along with the *zit-zit, zit-zit* of its flight call. The basic call is a *soo-weet.*

FOOD

Eats primarily seeds of coniferous and deciduous trees, plants and grasses. In summer insects make up an important part of the diet.

FAMILY LIFE

Monogamous pair; sometimes nests in loose colonies. The female builds a cup-shaped nest of woven fine twigs, grasses, lichens, mosses, fine rootlets, animal hair and feathers on a foundation of twigs placed in a low, dense bush or shrub such as a willow or dwarf birch. Occasionally it may be hidden in a rocky crevice. The typical clutch of 4 or 5 eggs is incubated by the female for 10 or 11 days. The altricial young remain in the nest for 9 to 14 days and are fed by both parents, mostly the female. One or 2 broods per year.

MIGRATION

Is an irruptive migrant that moves when the food supply (primarily tree seeds) in the North is scarce. In these alternating, irruptive years the species may move far south into southern Canada and the northern U.S. where it can be observed by humans. Otherwise, it is a bird of the northern tundra and taiga and goes largely unseen.

CONSERVATION CONCERNS

Species status overall in North America is *secure* in the United States and Canada.

RELATED SPECIES

One of 6 species in North America, including the redpolls, goldfinches and siskin, that belong to the genus *Carduelis*. Very similar in appearance, the hoary redpoll shares much of the ecology of the common redpoll and is difficult to distinguish from it.

AMERICAN GOLDFINCH

(*Carduelis tristis*)

Two American goldfinches scrapping in midair at a bird feeder in winter

This cheery little finch, ubiquitous throughout much of the continent, is unmistakable in its bright yellow and black plumage, and its habit of twittering during its roller-coaster flight.

APPEARANCE

Length: 5 inches. *Wingspan:* 9 inches. The male in breeding plumage is a brilliant yellow overall with black wings, tail and white wingbars; forehead and crown are black. The female is overall a dull yellow with black wings (though less strongly black than the male) and light wingbars. Nonbreeding adult is a plain brownish-yellow, making the sexes difficult to distinguish.

HABITAT

Open deciduous and riparian woodlands, overgrown fields with scattered woods, shrubs, orchards and hedgerows.

BEHAVIOR

In summer, goldfinches are usually seen in small flocks as they work their way through a weedy field gleaning seeds from dandelions, thistles and other common weeds. It normally feeds on or near the ground, but will also find food in alders, birches and other deciduous trees that produce small seeds. It also gets seeds from spruce cones. Flight is

The range of the American goldfinch

undulating with alternating flapping and gliding with wings held at the sides. Flight is usually accompanied by song. They form large flocks of up to 300 birds in winter. Is a common feeder bird in winter.

CALLS

The male's summer song is a spirited series of sweet lilting twitters and trills interjected with glissading *sweee* notes. The flight call is a distinctive *per-chick-o-ree, per-chick-o-ree,* sung on the downward flight glide.

FOOD

Is almost exclusively a seedeater, even when feeding young. Eats seeds of deciduous trees and shrubs, forbs, grasses, flower buds, berries and thistle-seeds. Will consume insects only rarely, usually in the spring. Shows a strong preference for black nyger seed at winter bird feeders.

FAMILY LIFE

Monogamous pair; one of the latest breeding songbirds, as nesting doesn't occur until late June or July when thistles begin flowering. The female builds a very tightly woven cup-shaped nest of plant stems, grass and bark, lined with plant down. Spider and caterpillar silk are often used in the construction of the nest, which is placed in the fork of a shrub or small tree from 3–20 feet above the ground. The typical clutch of 4 to 6 eggs is incubated by the female for 10 to 12 days. Altricial young remain in the nest for 11 to 17 days and are fed by both parents. One or 2 broods per year.

MIGRATION
Many populations overwinter, but birds that migrate generally arrive from mid-April to late May. Fall migration generally occurs from late October to mid-December.

CONSERVATION CONCERNS
Species status overall in North America is *secure* in the United States and Canada with a large, widely distributed population.

RELATED SPECIES
The American goldfinch is 1 of 6 tiny finches native to North America that belong to the genus *Carduelis*.

A male American goldfinch in jubilant song

LESSER GOLDFINCH

(Carduelis psaltria)

A brilliantly colored male lesser goldfinch has yet to achieve its full breeding plumage

This highly gregarious bird, often found in flocks of up to 400, is a common sight in certain areas of the American southwest.

APPEARANCE

Length: 4.5 inches. *Wingspan:* 8 inches. Smaller than the American goldfinch, the male has a black back (some birds have a medium olive green back), crown and forehead; bright white wingbars and patch at the base of the primary feathers; white tail patch; yellow underparts. Females have a drab green back and yellow underparts with faint white wingbars.

HABITAT
Lives in open habitats with shrubs, bushes, and scattered trees, and woods at the edges of streams and rivers.

BEHAVIOR
Its feeding habits are similar to the American goldfinch, foraging in small flocks in bushes, fields full of thistle or other seed-bearing plants and woodland edges.

The range of the lesser goldfinch

CALLS
The male's song is a rapid melodic twittering that includes phrases imitating other species, interspersed with distinctive *swee* notes. The song is somewhat lower and less flowing than that of the American goldfinch. The call is a clear *twui-yee*.

A male lesser goldfinch in breeding plumage

FOOD
Diet is largely of seeds of deciduous trees, grasses, forbs, berries and flower buds. Only rarely eats insects. Is a regular visitor to southwestern bird feeders.

FAMILY LIFE
Monogamous pair; the female builds a compact, woven cup-shaped nest of grass, plant stems, moss and bark, lined with plant down. The nest cradles a limb from 2–30 feet up in a tree or bush, or is occasionally placed in a tall weed. The usual clutch of 4 or 5 eggs is incubated by the female for 12 days. The altricial young remain in the nest for 11 to 15 days and are fed by both adults. One or 2 broods per year.

MIGRATION
Nonmigratory, permanent resident.

CONSERVATION CONCERNS
Species status overall in North America is *secure*. Capture of the species for the caged bird trade may be reducing populations in Central America.

RELATED SPECIES
One of 6 small finch species native to North America that belong to the genus *Carduelis*.

PINE SISKIN

(*Carduelis pinus*)

A pine siskin visiting a winter bird feeder

Because it follows the seed crops of the northern trees it depends on for food, this little forest finch might be found in great numbers in a given area one year only to disappear from it altogether the following year.

APPEARANCE

Length: 5 inches. *Wingspan:* 9 inches. Similar in size and shape to the American goldfinch, the male's upperparts are brown with dark streaking and underparts are somewhat lighter with dark streaking. Males have yellow wing markings that are conspicuous in flight and some males show a yellow wash on the sides. Females are a uniform brown with dark streaking and a very faint yellow wash. Both males and females have white wingbars, and the bill is more slender and pointed than that of the goldfinch or redpoll.

HABITAT

Is primarily a bird of coniferous and mixed deciduous-coniferous forests, but is also found in other woodlands, alders, shrubbery, shade trees and fields. Coniferous trees are preferred for nesting.

The range of the pine siskin

BEHAVIOR

Usually forages in flocks, even during the breeding season. Gleans seeds and insects from branches and foliage of trees. Generally feeds by starting high up in a tree and working downward as a group. Also feeds on the ground. Drinks sap from sapsucker drill holes. Is quite tame and easy to approach. Flocks, usually between 50 to 200, and occasionally up to 1,000 birds, are often mixed with other northern species. Flight is high, swift and undulating with alternating flapping and gliding with wings held against the body.

CALLS

The song is rapid series of trills and twitters with its call, a quickly rising *zreeeeee*, thrown in here and there for good measure. Sounds like the American goldfinch, but is huskier and more buzzy.

FOOD

Diet is largely plant-based and includes native coniferous and deciduous tree seeds, grass seeds, floral buds, flower nectar, sap and thistles. Also consumes insects during the spring and summer. Like the evening grosbeak, the siskin is strongly attracted to salt. During irruptive years it is common at bird feeders.

FAMILY LIFE

Monogamous pair; nests in loose colonies. The female builds a rather flat nest of twigs, grass, moss and tree bark, lined with animal hair, feathers and other soft materials such as thistle down and placed on a conifer branch well out from the trunk and off the ground. The typical clutch of 3 to 5 eggs is incubated by the female for 13 days. The altricial young remain in the nest for 15 days and are fed by both parents. Two broods per year.

MIGRATION

Is an irruptive migrant that moves south when the tree seed crops it depends on are poor, which usually occurs roughly every 2 years. When food is available, it will remain in the boreal forest. When migration does occur, birds usually arrive on breeding grounds between late February and May. Fall migration generally occurs between mid-August and November.

CONSERVATION CONCERNS

Species status overall in North America is *secure* in the United States and Canada. Despite this, numbers may have declined by half in recent decades.

RELATED SPECIES

Is 1 of 6 small finch species in North America that belongs to the genus *Carduelis*.

NORTHERN CARDINAL

(Cardinalis cardinalis)

A male northern cardinal is unmistakable in its brilliant red plumage

One of the most spectacular woodland birds of North America, the northern cardinal is expanding its range northward, particularly through the Northeast, where it is now common in places where it was once rare.

APPEARANCE

Length: 8.75 inches. *Wingspan:* 12 inches. Its plumage is unmistakable. The male is all red with a large distinctive crest, a long tail and a bold black mask. The female has a red-tipped crest, buff underparts, olive-brown upperparts, a partial dark mask, red bill and a red wash on the wings and tail.

HABITAT

Inhabits dense bushes, thickets, forest edges, tangled vegetation, usually located on the edge of an open area such as a field, stream, wetland, park or residential area. Shows a strong preference for deciduous vegetation over coniferous.

The range of the northern cardinal

BEHAVIOR

Forages on the ground by hopping along and picking up food. Also forages in trees and shrubs where it moves quickly along branches and twigs, capturing insects and eating seeds and buds. Uses its powerful bill for crushing and extracting seeds. Occasionally drinks sap from sapsucker holes. Visits bird feeders, particularly during early morning and near dusk. Flight is undulating with alternating flapping and gliding with wings pulled against the body.

Though not as boldly colored as the male, the female northern cardinal has a beauty all her own

CALLS
The cardinal utters a wide variety of beautiful, unmistakable songs. The most commonly heard song type is a series of clear musical whistled notes, *hurry-hurry-hurry* or *chew-chew-chew-chew* or *wet-year, wet- year, wet-year*. The female sings from the nest, perhaps to communicate to the male when she wants food. The call is a loud, metallic *chik*.

FOOD
Diet includes insects, caterpillars, small invertebrates such as snails and seeds, fruits and grains.

FAMILY LIFE
Monogamous pair; the female builds a compact, cup-shaped nest of tiny twigs, plant stems, bark, grass, leaves and rootlets, lined with soft material, and placed in the fork of a shrub or sapling, or in tangled branches, usually quite close to the ground. The typical clutch of 3 or 4 eggs is incubated mostly by the female for 12 or 13 days. Altricial young remain in the nest for 9 to 11 days and are fed mostly by the male. The male will continue to care for the young as the female lays and incubates another set of eggs. It is a prolific breeder, producing up to 4 broods per year.

MIGRATION
Year-round resident.

CONSERVATION CONCERNS
Species status overall for North America is *secure* in the United States and Canada. Appears to have benefited from human alteration of the landscape as forests have been opened up and the edge habitat the cardinal prefers has increased. This abundant bird has been expanding its range northward since the 1800s. It has been introduced to Bermuda, Hawaii and California.

RELATED SPECIES
Closest relative is the pyrrhuloxia, which belongs to the same genus *Cardinalis*.

The geographic ranges of bird species will change with time. Because they are so mobile and can adapt to changing environmental conditions, birds are able to respond somewhat more quickly to such demands than terrestrial animals. Many North American species have expanded or changed their range over the past number of decades. Species such as the northern cardinal and the tufted titmouse have moved northward in response to readily available food at bird feeders. In some cases range expansion can have a detrimental effect on species whose range is being newly exploited by an intruding species. For example, the movement of the barred owl into the Pacific northwestern United States may be pushing out the closely related endangered spotted owl. In the East, the expansion of the wood thrush into the far northeastern United States appears to be causing similar trouble for the closely related veery and hermit thrush.

PYRRHULOXIA

(Cardinalis sinuatus)

The pyrrhuloxia is similar to the northern cardinal in stature and shape

The strange name of this close relative of the cardinal is descriptive of the odd shape of its bill and is derived from the Greek words *pyrruos*, meaning "red" and *loxuos*, meaning "crooked."

APPEARANCE
Length: 8.75 inches. *Wingspan:* 12 inches. Similar in size and shape to the northern cardinal, the male is an overall gray with a prominent red crest, red face, belly and outer wing and tail feathers. The female is an overall buff color with a bit of red on outer wings, tail and crest. Both sexes have a long tail and a short, curved, somewhat parrot-like yellow bill.

HABITAT
Lives in southwestern riparian wood-lands, mesquite trees, thickets, thorn scrub and arid brushy areas.

BEHAVIOR
Forages like a cardinal by gathering food from the ground, and working its way among the twigs and foliage of veg-etation to glean insects and seeds. Spends more time off the ground than the cardinal. Although breeding territo-ries of the pyrrhuloxia and the cardinal often overlap, there is no evidence of conflict between them, despite occupying similar ecological niches. Flight is undulating with alternating flapping and gliding with wings pulled against the body. Associates with cardinals in mixed species flocks during fall and winter.

*The range of the
pyrrhuloxia*

CALLS
Songs are very similar to the northern cardinal's, although they tend to be shorter in duration, less musical and somewhat higher in pitch. The male sings from a prominent perch as it establishes its breeding territory. The call is a metallic *chik*.

FOOD
Diet includes insects, other invertebrates, berries, fruit and seeds such as mesquite beans.

FAMILY LIFE
Monogamous pair; the female builds a compact, cup-shaped nest of twigs, coarse grass and soft bark, lined by rootlets and plant fibers placed well off the ground in a bush, shrub or low tree. Typical clutch of 2 to 4 eggs is incubated by female for 12 to 14 days. Altricial young remain in the nest for 10 to 13 days and are fed by both parents. One or 2 broods per year.

The large crest and red mask and a small, parrot-like bill are hallmarks of the pyrrhuloxia

MIGRATION
Year-round resident.

CONSERVATION CONCERNS
Species status overall in North America is *secure* in the United States. Though still fairly common, it was at one time very common to abundant within its range. The destruction of millions of acres of scrubland in the southwestern United States has substantially reduced the pyrrhuloxia's habitat.

RELATED SPECIES
Its closest relative is the northern cardinal with which it shares the genus *Cardinalis*.

EVENING GROSBEAK

(Coccothraustes verspertinus)

A male evening grosbeak eating sunflower seeds at a feeder

This distinctive, large finch has seen a significant expansion of its breeding range to the east over the decades.

APPEARANCE
Length: 8 inches. *Wingspan:* 14 inches. The male has a dark brown head and nape with yellow eyebrows and forehead; yellow on back and breast; prominent white patch on wings. The female is overall a duller yellow with a gray head, face and back; white patches on the wings and chin. The large head, heavy conical bill and short tail are unmistakable on both sexes.

HABITAT

Lives in coniferous and mixed forests, treed parks and occasionally in suburbs. In cities in the eastern part of the continent, grosbeaks have benefited greatly from the planting of ornamental box elders whose seeds persist on the tree throughout the winter, thus providing food.

The range of the evening grosbeak

BEHAVIOR

Forages by gleaning food from the ground and from the foliage and twigs of trees. Its large bill is effective for cracking open the strong seeds that make up the largest part of its diet. Is quite tame; noisy and conspicuous during the nonbreeding season when it is found in large flocks. Is a common bird at winter bird-feeding stations. When not at feeders, it spends much of its time high up in the trees. Flies with an alternating flapping and gliding with wings held to the sides.

CALLS

The song is a series of abrupt musical warbles, ending in a high whistle. The call is a short *pleer*.

FOOD

Primary winter foods are seeds, fruits, berries and tree sap. During breeding season, evening grosbeaks eat insects, caterpillars and other invertebrates almost exclusively. Like other northern species of finches, it suffers high mortality in winter on highways as it seeks out road salt.

FAMILY LIFE

Monogamous pair; the female builds a loose, flimsy nest of sticks, twigs, rootlets and other plant matter, lined with rootlets and placed well out on a limb, usually high up in a conifer. The typical

A female evening grosbeak

clutch of 3 or 4 eggs is incubated by the female for 11 to 14 days. The altricial young remain in the nest for 13 to 14 days and are fed by both parents. One or 2 broods per year.

MIGRATION
Is considered an irruptive migrant, meaning that the species will migrate as it follows the food supply. In some years it may wander considerable distances, while at other times of high food availability it may move very little. The popularity of winter bird feeding has created an important food supply for the species. Will generally arrive on its breeding grounds between April and late May. Fall movement usually occurs between mid-July and mid-September.

CONSERVATION CONCERNS
Species status overall in North America is *secure* in the United States and Canada with the population having expanded eastward in historic times. Because it is not well studied, its population numbers are sketchy.

RELATED SPECIES
The sole member of the genus *Coccothraustes*, it is 1 of 16 species that regularly occur in North America that belong to the "true" finch family, *Fringillidae*.

EASTERN TOWHEE
(*Pipilo erythrophthalmus*)

An eastern towhee

This large, stocky member of the sparrow family, sometimes referred to as the "ground robin" and formerly called the "chewink," is normally a secretive bird that gives itself away when it performs its charming, whistled song.

APPEARANCE

Length: 8.5 inches. *Wingspan:* 10.5 inches. Males have a black back and head; white belly; rufous sides; a distinctive small wing patch on the wings; reddish eye, except for the southeastern race, which has a pale eye; conical, sparrow-like bill; long tail with white outer feathers. The female is similar except the head and back are brown.

HABITAT

Lives in dense, brushy habitats along the edge of forests, streams and rivers, roads, parks and other open areas. Will leave an area once a forest canopy develops.

BEHAVIOR

Towhee behavior closely resembles that of its sparrow relatives. Forages mostly on the ground by hopping and scratching with both feet at the same time to uncover food items in the leaf litter and humus. It will also glean insects from

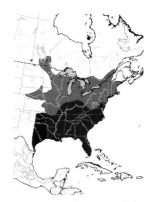

The range of the eastern towhee

the foliage and twigs of woody vegetation, especially during the breeding season. Sometimes runs quickly along the ground like a mouse or a vole. Its habit of remaining on or near the ground in dense vegetation has made it difficult to study. Flight is undulating with alternately flapping and gliding with wings pulled against the body.

CALLS

The song is a distinctive, clear, and musical three-note phrase, *think-of-meeee* with the last note being a trill. The call is a nasal *che-wink* or *too-wee*.

An male eastern towhee in a tangle of vegetation

FOOD
Diet includes insects, insect larvae, spiders and other invertebrates, small vertebrates such as salamanders, and grass and plant seeds, berries, acorns and fruit.

FAMILY LIFE
Monogamous pair; the female builds a nest of small twigs, leaves, bark and rootlets placed in a shallow depression on the ground. The rim of the nest is flush with the ground, usually sheltered by a small bush. Occasionally it will build a nest in a low tree or shrub no more than several feet off the ground. The typical clutch of 3 or 4 eggs is incubated by the female for 12 or 13 days. The altricial young remain in the nest for 10 or 12 days and are fed by both parents. Two or 3 broods per year.

MIGRATION
Southern populations are year-round residents. Northern birds usually arrive on their breeding grounds between mid-April and mid-May and generally migrate south in late September to October. It winters in the southern United States.

CONSERVATION CONCERNS
Species status overall in North America is *secure* in the United States and only *apparently secure* in Canada due to its restricted range there. Species is experiencing an overall decline throughout its range. This may be due to extensive browsing by an abundance of white-tail deer, which remove the dense understory the towhee needs to breed.

RELATED SPECIES
It is 1 of 6 towhees in North America belonging to the genus *Pipilo*. The spotted towhee and the eastern towhee were considered the same species until recently.

GREEN-TAILED TOWHEE

(Pipilo chlorurus)

A green-tailed towhee in its arid habitat

In spite of being somewhat common in its range throughout the western United States, the green-tailed towhee is poorly known because of its secretive, ground-loving nature.

APPEARANCE
Length: 7.25 inches. *Wingspan:* 9.75 inches. Overall looks like a large sparrow. Has bright olive green on wings and long tail; gray face and breast contrast with a bright white throat, white lores and a rufous crown.

HABITAT
Prefers dense thickets and low trees, shrublands, riparian scrub and disturbed open areas of mountain forests, including formerly burned-over areas.

BEHAVIOR

Forages by working through leaf litter and grasses on the ground using a hopping double-scratch method to uncover food with both feet simultaneously. Occasionally feeds in low bushes. Is very shy and generally will not tolerate being approached. Can be found by listening for its catlike *mew* call or its rustling of dry vegetation. Will often feed in small flocks during nonbreeding seasons.

The range of the green-tailed towhee

CALLS

The song, performed from a high perch, is a melodious series of jumbled short notes followed by short trills. Is similar to but more complex than the song of the fox sparrow. The call is a series of simple *mews*.

FOOD

Diet consists of mostly seeds, as well as berries, insects and insect larvae.

FAMILY LIFE

Monogamous pair; the female builds a nest of twigs, bark strips, grasses, hair and other fine plant materials on the ground or low in a shrub. The typical clutch of 3 or 4 eggs is incubated by the female for 11 to 13 days. The altricial young remain in the nest for 10 to 12 days and are fed by both parents. Two broods per year.

MIGRATION

Spring migrants usually arrive on breeding grounds between early April and late May. Fall migration generally occurs from late August to late October. Occasionally will delay migrating until December if the weather is mild and food is available.

A green-tailed towhee

CONSERVATION CONCERNS
Species status overall in North America is *secure* in the United States. Although it is difficult to determine population trends due to the secretive nature of the bird, it appears to be undergoing a slight decline, except in Oregon and the Wyoming Basin, where significant declines have been noted.

RELATED SPECIES
It is 1 of 6 species of towhee in North America, all of which belong to the genus *Pipilo*.

WHAT LIES AHEAD FOR NORTH AMERICA'S WOODLAND BIRDS?

The beauty and genius of a work of art may be reconceived, though its first material expression be destroyed; a vanished harmony may yet again inspire the composer; but when the last individual of a race of living things breathes no more, another heaven and another earth must pass before such a one can be again.

WILLIAM BEEBE

Rugged, primordial barrens stretch for miles in every direction on the highlands plateau of northern Cape Breton Island. Huge boulders dot the landscape, remnants of the last ice age. Inland, the stark wilderness rises gently to a distant horizon. Toward the sea, the land loses elevation gradually at first, then drops precipitously in spectacular cliffs and headlands into the Gulf of St. Lawrence, 1,500 feet below. This is a harsh land, subarctic in character due to its high elevation and latitude. The scant soil, short growing season, brutal winters and some of the fiercest winds on Earth result in relatively low biodiversity. The birds that nest here are hardy and well adapted to the harsh conditions. They include, among others, the gray jay, boreal chickadee, palm warbler and fox sparrow.

Below me, in a sheltered valley that was perhaps gouged out by a glacier 10,000 years ago, a chain of small boggy ponds glints in the summer sun. Surrounding them is a miniature forest of black spruce and white birch, most no more than 15 feet tall. I follow a trail down into the valley. It's late afternoon and a few resident birds are warming up their voices for evening song. A single urgent melody of liquid, musical trills rises up from a thicket near the water. I wait, then a few minutes later it comes again: a Lincoln's sparrow serenades from atop a spruce sapling only feet away. Just beyond it in a messy clump of living and dead trees, a Bicknell's thrush repeats a whispering, flute-like phrase, a bittersweet song if ever there was one, especially when heard in the lonely vastness of the highlands. One of the rarest of all North American woodland birds, this thrush finds its only breeding refuge in high, weather-beaten woods on remote scattered mountaintops throughout the northeastern part of the continent.

Despite their seeming removal from human influence, the Bicknell's thrush and other birds that breed in out-of-the-way places such as the Cape Breton Highlands and so many others, are far from being immune to the pressures brought to bear on natural ecosystems by humans. The fact is, our devastating reach extends in some way into every nook and cranny of bird habitat continent-wide, no matter where it is. On these very highlands, 30 years ago, tons of chemical insecticide was sprayed by airplanes to kill an infestation of spruce budworm for the pulp and paper industry. The ecosystem has apparently rebounded since then, but we'll never know how many birds and other organisms were killed or affected or if the natural community would be different today had the spraying not occurred.

A little farther north, the southern third of the boreal forest, which spans thousands of miles from the island of Newfoundland to Alaska, is being gobbled up by logging and agricultural expansion. One of the last great refuges of wilderness left anywhere on Earth is being frayed at the edges, impacting who knows how many of the billions of birds that breed there. Case in point: Is this industrial incursion the cause of the recent 98 percent population crash of the boreal-nesting rusty blackbird?

In the southeastern United States the destruction of swampy bottomland hardwood forests had long ago driven North America's only native parrot, the Carolina parakeet, to extinction. Other inhabitants of such woodlands, the ivory-billed woodpecker (evidence of its survival is inconclusive) and the Bachman's warbler, are also likely extinct now. The only 2 species remaining that are true bottomland/swamp forest habitat specialists in this part of the United States are the prothonotary warbler and the Swainson's warbler.

Birds that depend on the riparian woodlands of the southwestern United States are declining as these verdant green ribbons of riverside trees that meander across the desert are destroyed by

Some of our most beautiful birds are the woodland warblers, such as this black-throated green warbler in a white pine tree

development, grazing and the damming of rivers. The vermilion flycatcher, verdin and willow flycatcher have all experienced significant declines as their habitats shrink. Such insults to natural habitats are occurring widely throughout Canada and the United States. However, these may ultimately pale in comparison to a newly emerging threat to many of our woodland birds.

Global warming is already having a dramatic effect on North American birds. Because so much of their behavior, such as the timing of migration and nesting, is determined by seasonal and climatic cues, significant changes in species distribution are occurring. Warmer weather means many species migrate earlier in spring. This makes it harder for them to find insects to eat, so fewer and fewer young may survive. Seven species of wood warblers have significantly expanded their ranges northward over the past 25 years, putting them in competition with species already occupying those areas. This puts additional stress on *all* the species involved.

The predicted overall increase in the severity of hurricanes may kill countless birds directly during migration and destroy valuable forest habitat, especially in the southeastern United States. Based on computer modeling, in the near future, a number of state birds in the United States are expected to no longer live in the state that honors them because the climate there will be unsuitable. Up to 33 states could see American goldfinches disappear from summer woods and fields. The climate of northern and alpine areas appears to be warming at the quickest rate. This puts the countless birds that breed in the boreal region, as well as high-elevation species such as the Bicknell's thrush, at risk as their homes are transformed into places they are not adapted to survive in. At the opposite end of the continent, the southwestern United States may get hotter and drier, making what limited water that is available all the more precious to humans, perhaps at the expense of birds and other wildlife.

The litany of challenges facing woodland-dependent birds (in fact, *all* organisms) in North America is daunting. Problems appear to be at a scale way beyond what individuals or even groups of individuals can deal with. But no matter how one looks at climate change, habitat loss and every other threat to our bird life, one undeniable fact remains: They are caused by human activities. As one individual in the great collective of *Homo sapiens* responsible for these troubles, I am not proud. But I do take some solace in the fact that the challenges we face *are* human caused because at least we have some control over correcting or at least mitigating the problems that are presented. If we faced an imminent asteroid impact, a global spate of volcanic eruptions or widespread earthquakes, there would be nothing we could do but throw up our hands in resignation. But that is not the case with our current challenges. Let us find hope in the fact that the future of North America's woodland birds is in our hands. Conservation groups and resources involved in the protection of North American birds are listed at the back of the book.

SELECTED BIBLIOGRAPHY

Alsop, Jr., Fred J. *Birds of Canada*. Toronto: Dorling Kindersley Handbooks, 2002.

Armstrong, Edward A. *The Ethology of Bird Display and Bird Behavior*, rev. ed. New York: Dover Publications, 1965.

_____. *A Study of Bird Song*. New York: Dover Publications, 1973.

Askins, Robert A. *Restoring North America's Birds*. New Haven: Yale University Press, 2000.

Attenborough, David. *The Life of Birds*. Princeton: BBC Books, 1998.

Audubon, John James. *Audubon's Birds of America Popular Edition*. Toronto: The MacMillan Company, 1965.

Bent, Arthur Cleveland. *Life Histories of North American Birds of Prey, Part One*. New York: Dover Edition, 1961. Originally published in 1937.

Bent, A.C. *Life Histories of North American Flycatchers, Larks, Swallows and Their Allies*. Washington: U.S. Government Print Office, 1942.

Bent, A.C. *Life Histories of North American Wood Warblers*. Washington: U.S. Government Print Office, 1953.

Bent, A.C., et al. *Life Histories of North American Cardinals, Grosbeaks, Buntings, Towhees, Finches, Sparrows, and Allies*. Compiled and edited by Oliver L. Austin, Jr. New York: Dover, 1968.

Bird, David M. *The Bird Almanac*. Toronto: Key Porter Books, 1999.

Borror, Donald J. *Bird Song and Bird Behavior*. New York: Dover Publications, 1972.

Brooke, Michael, and Tim Birkhead. *The Cambridge Encyclopedia of Ornithology*. New York: Cambridge University Press, 1991.

Carwardine, Mark. *Birds in Focus*. London: Salamander Books, 1990.

Chapman, Frank M. *Bird Life*. New York: D. Appleton and Company, 1910.

Cornell Lab of Ornithology. *The Birds of North America Online*, 2004–2005. Ithaca: Cornell Lab of Ornithology, 2004–2005.

Douglas, Marjory Stoneman. *The Everglades: River of Grass*. Atlanta: Mockingbird Books, 1947.

Ehrlich, Paul R. *The Machinery of Nature*. New York: Touchstone Books, 1986.

_____, David S. Dobkin and Darryl Wheye. *The Birder's Handbook*. New York: Fireside, 1988.

Erskine, Anthony J. *Atlas of Breeding Birds of the Maritime Provinces*. Halifax: Nimbus/Nova Scotia Museum, 1992.

Feduccia, Alan. *The Origin and Evolution of Birds*, 2nd ed. New Haven: Yale University Press, 1999.

Fish and Wildlife Service. *Migration of Birds, Circular 16*. Washington: Fish and Wildlife Service, U.S. Dept. of the Interior, 1950.

Gill, Frank. *Ornithology*, 2nd ed. New York: W.H. Freeman & Company, 1995.

Godfrey, W. Earl. *The Birds of Canada*, rev. ed. Ottawa: National Museum of Natural Sciences, 1986.

Harrison, Hal H. *Birds' Nests*. Boston: Houghton Mifflin Company, 1975.

Heinrich, Bernd. *Mind of the Raven*. New York: Cliff Street Books, 1999.

_____. *Racing the Antelope*. New York: Cliff Street Books, 2001.

Jones, John Oliver. *Where the Birds Are*. New York: Morrow, 1990.

_____. *The U.S. Outdoor Atlas & Recreation Guide*. Boston: Houghton Mifflin Company, 1992.

Kaufman, Kenn. *Field Guide to North American Birds*. Boston: Houghton Mifflin, 2000.

Leopold, Aldo. *A Sand County Almanac*. New York: Oxford University Press, 1949.

Livingston, John A. *The Fallacy of Wildlife Conservation*. Toronto: McClelland & Stewart, 1981.

Marzluff, John M., and Rex Sallabanks. *Avian Conservation*. Washington: Island Press, 1998.

McElroy, Jr., Thomas P. *The Habitat Guide to Birding: A Guide to Birding East of the Rockies*. New York: Knopf, 1974.

Mountford, Guy. *Rare Birds of the World*. London: Collins, 1988.

National Wildlife Federation and American Bird Conservancy. *The Birdwatcher's Guide to Global Warming*. Washington: National Wildlife Federation & American Bird Conservancy, 2002.

NatureServe. 2006. *NatureServe Explorer: An Online Encyclopedia of Life [web application]*. Version 5.0. Arlington: NatureServe. Available at www.natureserve.org/explorer.

Peattie, Donald Culross. *Flowering Earth*. Compass Books, 1961.

Peterson, Roger Tory. *Eastern Birds*. Boston: Houghton Mifflin, 1980.

Poole, A., and F. Gill, eds. *The Birds of North America: Life Histories for the 21st Century*. Washington: The Birds of North America Inc., 1992.

Pough, Richard H. *Audubon Guides: All the Birds of Eastern and Central North America*. Garden City, NY: Doubleday, 1953.

Ridgely, R.S., et al. *Digital Distribution Maps of the Birds of the Western Hemisphere, version 1.0*. Arlington: NatureServe, 2003.

Robbins, Chandler S., Bertel Bruun, Herbert S. Zim, and Arthur Singer. *Birds of North America*, Exp. and rev. ed. New York: Golden, 1983.

Root, Terry. *Atlas of Wintering North American Birds: An Analysis of Christmas Bird Count Data*. Chicago: University of Chicago Press, 1998.

Sibley, David Allen. *The Sibley Guide to Birds*. New York: Knopf, 2000.

———. John B. Dunning, Jr., and Chris Elphick, eds. *The Sibley Guide to Bird Life & Behavior*. New York: Knopf, 2001.

Skutch, Alexander F. *Origins of Nature's Beauty*. Austin: The University of Texas Press, 1992.

_____. *The Minds of Birds*. College Station: Texas A&M University Press, 1996.

Stokes, Donald, and Lillian Stokes. *A Guide to Bird Behavior*, vols. 1, 2, 3. Boston: Little Brown, 1979, 1983, 1989.

Sutton, Clay, and Patricia Taylor Sutton. *How to Spot Hawks and Eagles*. Shelburne, VT: Chapters Publishing, 1996.

Teale, Edwin Way. *Green Treasury*. New York: Dodd, Mead & Company, 1952.

Thoreau, Henry David. *Thoreau on Birds*. Boston: Beacon Press, 1910.

Tudge, Colin. *The Variety of Life*. New York: Oxford University Press, 2000.

Tufts, Robie W. *Birds of Nova Scotia*, 3rd ed. Halifax: Nimbus Publishing/Nova Scotia Museum, 1961.

Weiner, Jonathan. *The Beak of the Finch*. New York: Vintage Books, 1994.

Wernert, Susan, ed. *North American Wildlife*. Pleasantville, NY: Reader's Digest Association, 1982.

SELECTED WOODLAND BIRDING AREAS IN CANADA

Below is a sample selection of places to observe woodland bird species in Canada. These sites were chosen because generally they are convenient, fruitful locations for observing some of the vast diversity of bird life that inhabits woodlands and forests. Many, many more sites exist, of course, and with a quick visit to the World Wide Web you can learn about a lot more of them.

AMHERST POINT MIGRATORY BIRD SANCTUARY
Canadian Wildlife Service
P.O. Box 6227
Sackville, NB
E4L 1G6
506-364-5044
website: www.ns.ec.gc.ca/wildlife/index.html

At just over 1,000 acres, federally protected Amherst Point near the Nova Scotia–New Brunswick border is one of the richest bird habitats in all of Atlantic Canada. Though known for its wetland species, the sanctuary boasts a high diversity of woodland birds for the region, found in the upland wooded areas, particularly during migration. Many woodland species, such as warblers and vireos, are found in the sanctuary's forests, one of which is a stand of old-growth hemlock. Over 200 species have been recorded at the site.

CAPE BRETON HIGHLANDS NATIONAL PARK
Ingonish Beach, NS
B0C 1L0
902-224-2306
website: www.pc.gc.ca/pn-np/cbreton/index.html

This large 366-square-mile park, one of the most spectacular in Canada, has recorded 229 species of birds. The threatened Bicknell's thrush breeds here and may be found along several of the park's trails. Boreal birds abound in the coniferous forests here, including the boreal chickadee, gray jay, spruce grouse and blackpoll warbler. Black-backed woodpecker may also be seen.

CAP TOURMENTE NATIONAL WILDLIFE AREA
570 ch.du Cap Tourmente
Saint Joachim, QC
G0A 3X0
418-827-4591
website: www.qc.ec.gc.ca/faune/faune/html/nwa_ct.html

Located on the beautiful north shore of the Saint Lawrence River, the 5,500-acre Cap Tourmente National Wildlife Area, famous as a key North American snow goose migratory stopover, is also an important area for woodland birds with 22 kinds of forest habitats. More than 300 species of birds have been recorded in the area, including the great grey owl, great horned owl, northern goshawk, yellow-rumped warbler, black-and-white warbler, red-eyed vireo and ruby-throated hummingbird, among others.

CYPRESS HILLS INTERPROVINCIAL PARK
Box 12, Elkwater, AB T0J 1C0
Alberta office: 403-893-3777
Box 850, Maple Creek, SK S0N 1N0
Saskatchewan office: 306-662-5411
website: www.se.gov.sk.ca/saskparks/

Jointly managed by the Alberta and Saskatchewan governments, this almost 50,000-acre island of forest in the grasslands is an important habitat for woodland birds. Some 220 species of birds have been recorded in the park, many of them species that are usually found in forests and foothills a substantial distance away to the north and to the west. Such birds include the yellow-rumped warbler, dusky flycatcher and ruby-crowned kinglet, among others. Over 100 species breed in the park.

FUNDY NATIONAL PARK
P.O. Box 1001
Alma, NB
E4H 1B4
506-887-6000
website: www.pc.gc.ca/pn-np/nb/fundy

This 80-square-mile park, located on the north shore of the Bay of Fundy in New Brunswick, protects some of the last wilderness in the province. Located on the Atlantic flyway and heavily forested with both coniferous and deciduous trees, some 260 species have been recorded in the park, with 95 breeding here. Ruffed grouse, dark-eyed junco, white-winged crossbills, boreal chickadee and many species of warblers, among others, are found here.

GROS MORNE NATIONAL PARK
Box 130
Rocky Harbour, NL
A0K 4N0
709-458-2417
website: www.pc.gc.ca/pn-np/nl/grosmorne/

One of the most awe-inspiring natural areas in North America, consisting of nearly 700 square miles of glacier carved fiords, mountains, plateaus, old-growth coniferous forest and coastline. The area has been designated a World Heritage Site by the United Nations. Two hundred thirty-nine species of birds have been recorded here, including 105 breeding species. Many northern specialities are found here including northern waterthrush, black-poll warbler, black-backed woodpecker, boreal chickadee and rock ptarmigan.

INGLEWOOD BIRD SANCTUARY
2425 9 Ave. SE, Calgary, AB
403-268-2489
website: www.bsc-eoc.org/national/ibs.html

This riparian sanctuary consists of approximately 80 acres located in the city of Calgary on the Bow River. Riverbank cottonwoods provide a haven in spring and summer for resident breeding woodland birds such as the western wood-pewee, northern flicker, least flycatcher and Baltimore oriole, as well as scores of migrating songbirds. In the fall, the sanctuary comes alive with up to 20 warbler species, including chestnut-sided, orange-crowned, magnolia, yellow-rumped, blackpoll, black-and-white and black-throated green warblers, among others. In winter, species such as black-capped chickadees, white-breasted nuthatches and great horned owls are found.

KEJIMKUJIK NATIONAL PARK
P.O. Box 236
Maitland Bridge, NS
B0T 1B0
902-682-2772
website: www.pc.gc.ca/pn-np/ns/kejimkujik/index

This 140-square-mile inland park of rolling forested hills and numerous lakes and streams has recorded 178 species within its boundaries. The park is made up of a combination of northern hardwood forests and conifers such as white pine and hemlock. The diverse woodlands attract many songbirds, including the 20 species of warblers that are known to breed in the park. Other notable breeding birds include pileated woodpeckers, downy and hairy woodpeckers and the barred owl, among others. Great-

crested flycatchers and wood thrush (both rare in the region) are
known to occur here.

LONG POINT PROVINCIAL PARK AND LONG POINT BIRD
OBSERVATORY
Box 99
Rowan, ON
NOE 1MO
519-586-2133
website: www.ontarioparks.com/english/long.html

This 25-mile-long sandspit jutting south into Lake Erie is a UN
Biosphere Reserve due to its importance to migratory birds. One of
the most important migratory stopover places in central North
America, some 370 species of birds, 173 of them breeding, have
been recorded throughout the peninsula. Species breeding on Long
Point include the endangered (in Canada) northern bobwhite,
ruffed grouse, eastern wood pewee, willow flycatcher, brown
creeper and 25 species of warblers.

PACIFIC RIM NATIONAL PARK
P.O. Box 280
Ucluelet, BC
VOR 3AO
website: www.pc.gc.ca/pn-np/bc/pacificrim/index_E.asp

Some 250 species of birds, mostly migrants, have been recorded in
this spectacular seashore park, located on the western side of
Vancouver Island. Thick, luxuriant rain forest supports the countless migrant songbirds that pass through in spring and fall while
traveling the Pacific migratory flyway. Breeding species total about
80 and include dark-eyed juncos, winter wrens, varied and
Swainson's thrushes, song sparrows, Stellar's jays, pileated woodpeckers, red crossbills and brown creepers.

POINT PELEE NATIONAL PARK
RR #1
Leamington, ON
N8H 3V4
519-322-2365 or 888-773-8888
website: www.pc.gc.ca/pn-np/on/pelee/index_E.asp

This world-famous birding site is considered one of the best in North America. Consisting of 8 square miles located on the tip of a long peninsula jutting into Lake Erie, Point Pelee is the most southerly point in Canada and consists of one of the few remaining undisturbed eastern deciduous forests in the country. Several woodland species are at the northern limit of their breeding ranges here, including the yellow-breasted chat, Acadian flycatcher, red-bellied woodpecker, Carolina wren and blue-gray gnatcatcher. Some 370 species have been recorded, among them 42 species of wood warblers.

PRINCE EDWARD POINT BIRD OBSERVATORY AND NATIONAL WILDLIFE AREA
Prince Edward Point Bird Observatory
Picton, ON
website: www.peptbo.ca

Prince Edward Point National Wildlife Area, located near Picton, Ontario, is a narrow spit of land jutting south into Lake Ontario. It has the highest concentration of migratory birds of the Canadian side of the lake. More than 300 species, most of them migratory, have been recorded in the area, a major staging point for birds heading north in spring and south again in fall. It is especially productive during spring songbird migration when scores of species of warblers, vireos, flycatchers and thrushes are present. In fall, up to 2,000 raptors can be observed passing through.

RIDING MOUNTAIN NATIONAL PARK
Wasagaming, MB
R0J 2H0
204-848-7275
website: pc.gc.ca/pn-np/mb/riding/index_E.asp

This nearly 1,200-square-mile park is an island of boreal forest, mixed forest and grasslands surrounding by a sea of agricultural land. It is a crossroads where ecosystems of the east, west and north meet to create a natural tapestry of habitats for birds. Approximately 262 species of birds have been recorded here, including breeding species such as the red-tailed hawk, ruffed grouse, northern hawk-owl, ruby-throated hummingbird, alder flycatcher, hermit thrush, chestnut-sided warbler, orange-crowned warbler and purple finch.

RONDEAU PROVINCIAL PARK
RR #1
Morpeth, ON
N0P 1X0
519-674-1750
website: www.rondeauprovincialpark.ca

Yet another superb birding site on Lake Erie, Rondeau is an 8,000-acre park located on a long sandspit. The eastern deciduous forest here is made up of beech, shag-bark hickory, tulip-tree and sugar maple among others. Some 340 species of birds have been recorded, 140 of which breed, including the yellow-breasted chat and prothonotary warbler.

SELECTED WOODLAND BIRDING AREAS IN THE UNITED STATES

Below is a sample selection of places to observe woodland bird species in the United States. These sites were chosen because generally they are convenient, fruitful locations for observing some of the vast diversity of bird life that inhabits woodlands and forests. Many, many more sites exist, of course, and with a quick visit to the World Wide Web you can learn about a lot more of them.

ACADIA NATIONAL PARK
P.O. Box 177
Eagle Lake Road
Bar Harbor, ME 04609-0177
207-288-3338
website: www.nps.gov/acad

Acadia National Park comprises over 40,000 acres of rugged coastal landscape on the coast of northern Maine. Positioned between the coniferous forests to the north and the eastern deciduous forest to the south, Acadia is a land of transition where species from both zones mingle. Over the years, the gradual transition of more southerly birds into the park has been noted. Some 338 species of birds have been recorded in the park, including 23 species of breeding warblers, making it one of the top birding spots in the United States.

BIG THICKET NATIONAL PRESERVE
Headquarters:
6044 FM420
Kountze, TX 77625
409-951-6725
website: www.nps.gov/bith/

This "biological crossroads" in eastern Texas consists of 4 distinct ecosystems: eastern deciduous forest, coastal plain, arid southwest and central plains. Nearly 100,000 acres in extent, over 300 species of birds have been recorded there, including the last confirmed sighting ever of the now probably extinct ivory-billed woodpecker in May 1971 (a 2005 report of the species surviving in Arkansas remains controversial). Woodland birds, both migratory and breeding, such as warblers, vireos, thrushes, woodpeckers and nuthatches abound along the many birding trails in the preserve.

BOGUE-CHITTO NATIONAL WILDLIFE REFUGE
61389 Hwy. 434
Lacombe, LA 70445
985-882-2000
website: www.fws.gov/boguechitto

One of the most pristine swampland forests remaining in the United States, this wilderness is located just 30 miles northwest of New Orleans and comprises 36,000 acres of hardwood floodplain, cypress-tupelo brakes and numerous sloughs and bayous. Approximately 150 species of birds, including a variety of warblers, use the area both for breeding and during migration.

CAPE MAY NATIONAL WILDLIFE REFUGE
24 Kimbles Beach Road
Cape May Courthouse, NJ 08210-2078
609-463-0994
website: www.capemay.fws.gov

Located in coastal New Jersey, on Delaware Bay, this is one of the most famous bird sites in the United States. 317 species of birds have been recorded over the refuge's 11,000 acres. The primary woodland area is in the Great Cedar Swamp Division, which consists of a hardwood swamp and eastern white cedar. Migrants linger on the peninsula before the long journey across Delaware Bay. Nearly 100 species of neotropical migrant birds have been recorded. It is a great fall raptor migration site.

CORKSCREW SWAMP SANCTUARY
375 Sanctuary Rd. West
Naples, FL 34120
239-348-9151
website: www.corkscrew.audubon.org

This beautiful Audubon sanctuary, located in the very southern part of Florida, is an 11,000-acre wilderness that is home to one of the largest stands of old-growth bald cypress left in North America. Some of the trees are over 700 years old. A haven for wetland birds, Corkscrew is also an important nesting site for woodland birds, including the red-shouldered hawk, eastern screech-owl, pileated woodpecker, great crested flycatcher and blue-gray gnatcatcher, among others.

CORONADO NATIONAL FOREST
300 W. Congress St.
Tucson, AZ 85701
520-388-8300
website: www.fs.fed.us/r3/coronado

Covering about 1.8 million acres of southeast Arizona and southwest New Mexico, Coronado National Forest ranges in elevation from 3,000 feet on the desert to nearly 11,000 feet in high alpine zones. This range of elevations results in a wide bird diversity and supports vegetation types that can be found from Mexico to Canada. Famous birding hot spots, such as Cave Creek Canyon, near Portal, Arizona, boasts rich bird diversity. It is a center for hummingbird diversity in the United States.

CROSS CREEKS NATIONAL WILDLIFE RESERVE
643 Wildlife Road
Dover, TN 37058
931-232-7477
website: www.fws.gov/crosscreeks

Twenty-five percent or 2,500 acres of this reserve near the Tennessee-Kentucky border consists of deciduous woodlands. The area is a haven for woodpeckers. The northern flicker, red-bellied, downy and hairy woodpeckers breed here, and the yellow-bellied sapsucker and pileated woodpecker are occasionally seen. The woods are an important migratory stopover site for a large variety of warblers, vireos and sparrows. Approximately 250 species of birds have been recorded in the reserve.

DERBY HILL BIRD OBSERVATORY
P.O. Box 2894
Syracuse, NY 13220-2894
website: www.derbyhill.org

This reserve, located on the southeast shore of Lake Ontario, may be only 60 acres in size, but it nevertheless one of the premier places in the United States to observe migratory birds. Over 40,000 hawks are counted migrating through the area in spring, as well as thousands of songbirds such as nuthatches, American robins, cedar waxwings and finches. Later in spring further hordes of warblers, vireos and orioles can be seen migrating through.

GILA NATIONAL FOREST
3005 E. Camino del Bosque
Silver City, NM 88061
505-388-8201
website: www2.srs.fs.fed.us/r3/gila/

This is one of the largest wilderness areas left in the lower 48 states. The 3.3 million acres in southcentral New Mexico range from the semidesert at 3,000 feet elevation with oak, juniper and cactus to high cool mountain environments with aspen and Douglas fir. Almost 350 bird species have been recorded and nearly 170 breed here. A rich riparian habitat is found (among other spots in the national forest) in the Gila River Bird Habitat Area.

GREAT SWAMP NATIONAL WILDLIFE REFUGE
241 Pleasant Plains Rd.
Basking Ridge, NJ 07920
973-425-1222
website: www.fws.gov/northeast/greatswamp/

The Great Swamp National Wildlife Refuge has 7,600 acres of varied habitats, including swamp hardwoods, upland forest, hardwood ridges and wetlands. Both southern and northern botanical zones are represented in the refuge and include oak, beech and mountain laurel. Two hundred forty-four recorded species of birds include about 100 breeding species such as the great-crested flycatcher, willow flycatcher, eastern phoebe, tufted titmouse and red-eyed, white-eyed and yellow-throated vireos. A variety of wood warblers utilize the area during migration.

GREEN SWAMP PRESERVE
c/o The Nature Conservancy
131 Racine Drive, Suite 101
Box number 5
Wilmington, NC 28403
910-395-5000
website: www.nature.org

Located in the far southern part of North Carolina, the Nature Conservancy's Green Swamp Preserve consists of nearly 16,000 acres of the continent's finest long-leaf pine savannas and dense evergreen shrub poscasins. The preserve is inhabited by the endangered red-cockaded woodpecker.

KIRTLAND'S WARBLER WILDLIFE MANAGEMENT AREA
Administered by the Seney National Wildlife Refuge
1674 Refuge Entrance Rd.
Seney, MI 49883
906-586-9851
website: www.fws.gov/midwest/seney

Established to protect the Kirtland's warbler, one of the most endangered birds in the United States, this management area is located in the northern part of Michigan's lower peninsula. It consists of nearly 7,000 acres in 119 individual sites located in eight different counties where the bird breeds. The population has increased from a low of only 200 singing males (the easiest way to census the bird is to count the number of singing males) in the 1970s to about 1,200 now.

PATAGONIA-SONOITA CREEK PRESERVE
c/o Ramsey Canyon Preserve
27 Ramsey Canyon Rd.
Hereford, AZ 85615
520-378-4952
website: www.nature,org

Located in a rich flood plain in southern Arizona, this Nature Conservancy preserve comprises over 300 acres of rich riparian woodland of Fremont cottonwoods and Goodding willow that runs along one of the few permanent streams in the region. Over 275 species of birds have been recorded, including a large variety of migrating warblers and some 22 species of flycatchers, including the vermilion flycatcher.

POINT REYES NATIONAL SEASHORE
1 Bear Valley Rd.
Point Reyes Station, CA 94956
415-464-5100
website: www.nps.gov/pore

This 71,000-acre peninsula with its cliffs, beaches, estuaries and forests, located north of San Francisco, boasts the highest avian diversity of any national park in the U.S. Situated on the Pacific migratory flyway, some 490 species have been recorded here.

SENEY NATIONAL WILDLIFE REFUGE
1674 Refuge Entrance Rd.
Seney, MI 49883
906-586-9851
website: www.fws.gov/midwest/seney

Consisting of 95,000 acres located on the Upper Peninsula of Michigan, this refuge is a mixture of wetland and woodland habitats, including large stands of red pine. Over 200 species of birds have been recorded and 135 species nest here, including Canada, chestnut-sided, yellow, magnolia and black-and-white warblers, as well as other woodland birds such as the ruffed grouse, red-eyed vireo and hermit thrush.

ST. MARK'S NATIONAL WILDLIFE REFUGE
P.O. Box 68
St. Mark's, FL 32355
850-925-6121
website: www.fws.gov/saintmarks/

Located on the Florida panhandle, St. Mark's is largely wetland, but includes important upland areas of oak and pine forests, palm hammocks and hardwood swamps. The endangered red-cockaded woodpecker inhabits the refuge and some 250 species of birds have been recorded here, including vireos, warblers and flycatchers, among others.

WOODBOURNE FOREST AND WILDLIFE SANCTUARY
c/o The Nature Conservancy
Hauser Nature Center
P.O. Box 55, Long Pond Rd.
Long Pond, PA 18334
570-643-7922
website: www.nature.org/wherewework/northamerica/
pennsylvania

Located in northeastern Pennsylvania, this Nature Conservancy sanctuary consists of 654 acres of forest, some of it the oldest-growth forest left in the northeastern part of the state. A stand of ancient hemlocks and hardwoods date to the seventeenth century. The sanctuary is a mosaic of forests and streams with an elevation change of over 300 feet. Neotropical migrant songbirds such as warblers are common in the sanctuary. The Blackburnian, black-throated green and Canada warblers, brown creeper and blue-headed vireo are a few of these birds that breed here, as well as larger species such as the pileated woodpecker, great horned owl and red-tailed hawk.

WOODLAND BIRDS INTERNET RESOURCES

Below are names and website addresses for a selection of organizations that are involved in bird conservation and birding in North America. All of these are great organizations that carry out crucial conservation work and they deserve our support. Some of the websites, especially those of NatureServe, BirdSource and the Cornell Laboratory of Ornithology, are great learning resources, offering an astonishing amount of information about birds' natural history and their conservation.

AMERICAN BIRD CONSERVANCY
www.abcbirds.org

AMERICAN BIRDING
ASSOCIATION
www.americanbirding.org

BIRDLIFE INTERNATIONAL
www.birdlife.net

BIRDSOURCE
www.birdsource.org

BIRD STUDIES CANADA
www.bsc-eoc.org

BOREAL SONGBIRD INITIATIVE
www.borealbirds.com

CANADIAN BOREAL INITIATIVE
www.borealcanada.ca

CANADIAN NATURE FEDERATION
www.cnf.ca/bird

CORNELL LABORATORY OF
ORNITHOLOGY
www.birds.cornell.edu

NATIONAL AUDUBON SOCIETY
www.audubon.org

NATURESERVE
www.natureserve.org

NORTH AMERICAN BIRD
CONSERVATION INITIATIVE
www.nabci.net

PARTNERS IN FLIGHT
www.partnersinflight.org

ACKNOWLEDGMENTS

Thank you to Paula Leslie for her continued support, as well as her assistance in the field.

Thanks to Dick and Sharon Nelson for facilitating getting photos of certain southwestern species.

Thanks to Bernard Forsythe for revealing his secret goshawk site all those years ago.

Thanks to NatureServe for once again granting permission to use its western hemisphere range maps and distribution maps. Range map data was provided by NatureServe in collaboration with Robert Ridgely, James Zook, The Nature Conservancy—Migratory Bird Program, Conservation International—CABS, World Wildlife Fund—US, and Environment Canada—WILDSPACE.

Thanks to John Rose of Two Rivers Wildlife Park in Cape Breton, NS

Thanks to Michael Mouland and the staff of Key Porter Books for their support of this project.

INDEX